WORD BY WORD

MARILYN MCENTYRE

WORD
by
WORD

A *Daily Spiritual* Practice

WILLIAM B. EERDMANS
PUBLISHING COMPANY
Grand Rapids, Michigan

WM. B. EERDMANS PUBLISHING CO.
2140 Oak Industrial Drive N.E., Grand Rapids, Michigan 49505
www.eerdmans.com

22 21 20 19 18 17 16   1 2 3 4 5 6 7

Library of Congress Cataloging-in-Publication Data

Names: McEntyre, Marilyn Chandler, 1949- author.
Title: Word by word: a daily spiritual practice / Marilyn McEntyre.
Description: Grand Rapids: Eerdmans Publishing Company, 2016.
Identifiers: LCCN 2016019029 | ISBN 9780802873866 (pbk.: alk. paper)
Subjects: LCSH: Meditations. | Vocabulary—Miscellanea. |
Language and languages—Religious aspects—Christianity.
Classification: LCC BV4832.3 .M3484 2016 | DDC 242—dc23
LC record available at https://lccn.loc.gov/2016019029

The poem "Prayer" by Galway Kinnell, which appears in "Sunday: Enjoy
the Moment," is from The Past. Copyright © 1985 by Galway Kinnell.
Reprinted by permission of Houghton Mifflin Harcourt Publishing
Company. All rights reserved.

CONTENTS

INTRODUCTION

A while ago I was driving one of my favorite four-year-olds to the public library, chatting with him about what we might find there. He asked if he could play word games on the computers in the children's section. I said he could do that if a computer was available. He was quiet for a few moments; then I heard him mumbling to himself contentedly, "Available. Available. Available." Apparently the word appealed to him.

I smiled, knowing how the sound and "taste" of a certain word can sometimes surprise me into sudden pleasure in the midst of conversation. I'll find myself turning the word over and over in my mind like a beach pebble that glimmers in sea water and summons the eye to closer inspection.

When a word calls particular attention to itself in that way, it awakens associations, memories, reflections. One instance I remember vividly is an encounter I had with the word "dwell." I was reading the opening line of Psalm 91: "He who dwells in the shelter of the Most High will abide in the shadow of the almighty." It's a line I had loved for years, but this time the word "dwell" moved for a moment into the foreground, and I found myself lingering over it, struck by something gentle and kind and hospitable about the quality of at-homeness it suggests.

Over time I found that my experience is a common one: sometimes a word floats into mind like a few notes from a familiar tune and stays a while. You find yourself hearing it with noticeable frequency, using it a little more consciously, and carrying it through the day. It's good to pay attention to these words when they come, usually in the course of reading a passage of Scripture or a poem, a new book or the daily paper. It's good to consider what stories and teachings the words bring with them, what kinds of questions attach to them, what they evoke and invite.

This series of meditations on single words is an invitation to dwell with and reflect on a single word over the course of a week, to consider one word used seven different ways, in seven different phrases. In this process you recall the word's personal, biblical, and sometimes literary contexts, consider experiences the word brings up, how your use or sense of it has changed over time, how it has acquired new layers of meaning. And you allow the word to become a focus for prayer and meditation.

A week allows spacious time for layers of meaning and memory to unfold. Each day we may turn the same word to a new angle, find it in a different poem or passage, be more attentive to it in conversation, turn it to new purposes. The practice of living with a single word for a week can become a complement to centering prayer and to *lectio divina*, allowing us to hear that word in new ways, and allow it to invite us into new places of the heart.

Both these time-honored practices, *lectio divina* and centering prayer, remind us of the power of a single word or phrase to open a window or a path, incite an epiphany or an insight, or let in a rush of feeling we didn't know had been buried in a deep place. The one practice leads to the other. In *lectio divina* we listen as we read a passage from Scripture for a word or phrase that summons us to pause and hear the voice of the Spirit. That word or phrase becomes a focal point for the reading that day—a new avenue of grace discovered even in the heart of a very familiar passage. In centering prayer we begin with a "sacred word" that quiets and focuses the mind and gradually dispels the clutter of preoccupations and internal chatter. This word gathers silence around it, silence in which we may become newly aware of divine presence.

My hope is that this collection of reflections on single words will encourage you to experiment with these practices and extend them into daily life by "carrying" a particular word with you for a whole week—one that has been given to you and that brings with it, if you let it, a cascade of thoughts and feelings worth exploring. I offer these words in the spirit in which one monastic brother would ask another to "give me a word" to provide focus and direction. As you listen for the "word" spoken to you, you will very likely find that more words emerge as you need them.

Dwelling, lingering, pondering, listening, praying—these are all countercultural practices. They slow us into a silence that has to be reclaimed, sometimes with fierce intention, from the noise and haste and forward momentum of daily life. Many of us have normalized busyness to the point of chronic overload. Staying with, being still, and coming back rather than going on are spiritual survival disciplines on the choppy seas of distraction.

The words in this volume come from my own meditations, from morning readings of Scripture, from poems read at bedtime, from conversations where suddenly I've noticed and heard words in a new way. Each of them has taken its place as a key term in my spiritual lexicon and, I would say, my personal theology. Returning to them focuses my faith and equips me as I continue the journey.

As it happens, the words in this volume are all verbs. Though I didn't initially plan it that way, I recognize that verbs are a good place to start. They're the fulcrum of every sentence, and the keys to many kinds of seeking. "Receive," "enjoy," and "ask" offer invitation and direction and a little nudge to move into the day and act in the world with renewed focus and life-giving energy. A few of the verbs are phrases: "let go" and "be still" arrive with the force and conviction of imperatives that are also promises rooted in two ancient, holy words by which all creation was spoken into being: "Be" and "Let." In the story of creation and of God's work with humankind, verbs have a special place and power.

The choice of words and the sequence in which they occur here have no necessary logic, though you may see in the table of contents some alternation between invitation and challenge, between receptivity and activity. But I invite you to read the words in any order, allowing the table of contents itself to be a little exercise in noticing where your interests, desires, and life currents lead you as you open the book on any given day. In spending time with these words, allowing them to awaken mind and spirit, I have found each of them to be a way into the "interior castle." Each of them has offered its own singular teaching.

I hope these reflections will encourage you as you pursue your own practices of word work and word play. And if you haven't developed such practices, I invite you to discover, as I have, to my lasting delight, how words may become little fountains of grace. How a single word may become, for a time, "equipment for living." How a single word may open wide wakes of meaning and feeling. How a single word may, if you hold it for a while, become a prayer.

Listen

. . . for the guidance you need

. . . for the need behind the words

. . . into the silences

. . . as an act of participation

. . . through the noise to the music

. . . courageously

. . . when you pray

Sunday: Listen for the guidance you need

"Christ in mouth of friend and stranger," St. Patrick reminds us in his ancient prayer that enumerates the many ways Christ may be present to us. God's guidance comes most often from human sources, but only if we listen for it. "Notice what you notice," I suggest to my students as they read.

This is also a good practice for those times when a word we need to hear comes up "randomly" in a casual conversation. Or when a friend summons the courage to broach a delicate topic. Or when a child asks an uncomfortable question. Notice the images and phrases and sentences that come to you in periods of silent prayer or meditation. Notice where irritations arise in the midst of daily living together, and where you feel suddenly affirmed.

The obvious sources of guidance are reliable—common sense, Scripture, family members who know us all too well, friends, leaders, and teachers with proven competence and compassion. Less obvious are the subtle ways the Spirit summons us to attention, breaking into conversations that have become routine with a new word of life, bringing us up short with someone's objection to an unexamined assumption. When we listen for guidance, we listen differently, more humbly, more openly.

A wise woman once told me, "Listen for God's voice everywhere. And don't forget that the Spirit may use the people who annoy you to teach you." Precisely the word we need may come from a sullen nineteen-year-old with a nose ring, or from the bore who corners us at a party, or from an officious neighbor. If we listen widely and willingly—not indiscriminately, but with the intention of discerning what may help direct our steps and hone our choices—our lives will be rich with surprises.

Listening like this consistently takes practice. Listening beyond our resistances and prejudices (can any good thing come out of Nazareth—or from the other side of the aisle?) may lead us into territory where our assumptions may at least be examined, and our conclusions modified.

———

Monday: Listen for the need behind the words

In his book on non-violent communication, Marshall Rosenberg emphasizes the importance of listening for the need that lies behind an accusation or a complaint or a demand. When I respond to someone's request or criticism or out-of-the-blue observation, I may not pick up on the need for approval or reassurance or permission or validation that remains unstated. Listening for what lies behind the obvious message requires discipline and deliberation. And it is a skill that works to good effect only if it's exercised with humility: we cannot presume to know for certain another's unnamed needs. But we can try to discern them.

Good listening requires imagination. To hear what isn't being said, I may have to piece together story fragments. I may have to ask, "What memories come up when we talk about this?" "Does this problem have a history?" "When have you felt like this before?"

When a child tells me three times in close succession (as one recently did), "I really like that pretty deck of cards you have," it doesn't take much imagination to figure out that she wants me to give them to her. But behind that immediate want may lie a need to learn how to navigate the space between graciousness and greed where desires are met or modified. When an adult tells me (as one recently did), "You're just the person we want for this job," I can succumb to well-placed flattery, or I can pause long enough to imagine something more complex at work—perhaps a need to end a time-consuming search or to recruit me as an ally or to please someone higher up the ladder.

I'm not saying that we cannot or should not ever take each other's words at face value. Especially in communities of faith where we strive to "let our yes be yes and our no be no," it would be disingenuous and unkind to always look for hidden motives or meanings. But to see one another as people with authentic needs, and to recognize that those needs are as real as hunger and thirst and deserve our attention, is to pause long enough to acknowledge how intricate is the design of our psyches and how deep are the untended corners of our hearts.

We can practice listening for the needs and the hopes and the expectations that others bring into conversation by creating safe spaces in which the questions can be asked simply and openly: "What do you need?" "Why might this be on your mind?" "Do you know why this situation might feel so threatening?" "What are the fears that make you hesitate?" These aren't the stuff of polite patter, but life-giving questions to be broached gently, prayerfully, and in due time.

———

Tuesday: Listen into the silences

Quiet is hard to come by. As we adapt to incessant ambient noise and media chatter, even the impulse to seek quiet can atrophy. Noise can provide protection from painful memories and from unbidden and unwelcome thoughts. Most of my students freely admit to doing their work with the radio on—or their 500 favorite iTunes. Some need electronic noise to fall asleep.

I remember a conversation with a classmate who, when I suggested we needed a little silence each day to "go inside," asked in mock horror, "Why would anyone want to do that? It's dark in there!" And so it is at times. But that darkness may offer rest from the brassy sound-and-light shows that tire the senses. It is surely one of those places the Psalmist assures us God will meet us: "Even the darkness is not dark to you . . . for the darkness is as light to you." It is in silence that God often speaks most clearly.

Every tradition teaches some form of contemplative practice that quiets the mind. The objective of those simple yet strenuous practices is to open oneself to divine address. Centering prayer, rosaries, and sitting meditations train the faithful in a quality of attention that does not come naturally to most of us. Sometimes into that silence a sentence comes: "You don't need to be afraid." "Let go." "Wait and watch." Sometimes only a word or phrase: "heart's desire," "sure and certain," "courage," "peace." Sometimes a feeling: full-hearted forgiveness or delight or a pure sorrow that releases us from bitterness. Silence allows the silt to settle so we can see what gleams and swims below the surface.

Not only in our private devotions but in our shared lives we need to create still places where the arguing stops, and the bargaining and the exchange of news, so that we can listen together and receive direction. In Deuteronomy, Moses says to the gathered people, "Be silent, O Israel, and listen! You have now become the people of the Lord your God. Obey the Lord your God. . . ." "Listen" and "obey" share a common root: to do one is to do the other.

Distracted and burdened as they may become by maintenance costs and bickering committees and competing commitments, churches can still open sacred spaces and provide a silence in which renewal and refreshment are possible. They can strive to maintain liturgical silences into which a dozen or a hundred or a thousand people can listen together for the voice of the God who calls them by name.

"The Lord is in his holy temple," Habakkuk writes. "Let all the earth be silent before him." Into that silence God moves to meet us, and in it God speaks to a people willing to listen.

Wednesday: Listen as an act of participation

As a long-time teacher, I try to get all my students to "participate" in classes where discussion is one of the skills to be honed. I tell them that participation in class discussion counts as part of their grade. I call on them by name. This is basic pedagogy: students need to practice entering public discussion and accounting for their opinions.

But then came the alumni day when I ran into a former student. As I recalled, she sat at the back of the class, put her head down over her notes, and said almost nothing. I heard barely a word out of her all semester. She wrote good papers, but I assumed that was simply because she happened to be a good writer, not because she was learning anything I had to teach. At the alumni gathering, though, she stopped me with a broad smile to tell me what a turning point that class had been for her. She said it had helped her to realize her gifts and change her reading habits. I went home marveling. Who knew? Her participation had been simply to listen intently to the conversation, to take it to heart and allow it to change her.

Some people share their opinions freely; others say nothing because they aren't invested in the conversation. But those who really listen, consider, take time to ponder, and act in response to what they hear—they are rare and valuable participants in the life of any community. They're not avoiding responsibility when they wait to offer an opinion; they're allowing themselves to be receptacles. They become sites of germination—good soil where seed may break open and yield its fruit in good time.

In Greek the word for participation is *koinonia,* which may also be translated as "communion by intimate participation." Good listeners help create that intimacy. People seek them out to speak their hearts. They are often the ones who, without imposing their own agendas, ask questions that need to be asked. One gifted listener I know is a pastoral caregiver who asks very simple questions like "What is that like for you?" He pays close attention to the answer. Then he asks the next question. Part of his role is to slow people down. "Take your time," he says, and he means it.

How little we hear about most of Jesus' disciples in the course of the Gospel narratives! What we know about them—the ones whose names appear hardly at all—is that they followed and they listened. What they heard empowered them to become leaders and martyrs whose lives offered models of courage and faith.

Among Jesus' female followers, one of the most beloved is Mary, whose listening—the "better part" she chose—lay at the heart of her participation in Jesus' life and ministry. Her story reminds us that it may be the quiet listeners among us who are harboring gifts greater than we imagine, gifts that sustain the life of the whole Body.

Thursday: Listen through the noise to the music

My husband and I rarely eat out anymore; it's too noisy. The sound of two dozen conversations in one room makes it hard to have our own. Most of us who move about in the world live in the midst of noises that keep us in a state of chronic distraction, no matter how good we become at screening them out. But if we listen past the noise, we may hear healing music—even though it can be harder to find. Naturalists say that most of us in North America live in areas where the wildlife population is reduced to less than 20 percent of what it once was. We haven't managed to eliminate birdsong from cities, but we've come tragically close.

As I've grown older, I've noticed how many folks who retire take up gardening or "birding." As the preoccupations of institutional life diminish, many seek out what they've missed: encounters with the earth and its creatures. The beauty of beasts and birds. The sounds of children playing. Waves. Windy hills. The privilege of a new season of leisure allows them to listen differently and to hear the music that was always there, underneath the noise and the haste.

It takes time to listen to music. It sets its own pace. The wood thrush sings as long as it needs to, whether we're listening or not. The act of obedience required in "birding" is to stop long enough to hear the whole cycle of song, perhaps to see the bird through the leaves, and to listen past the whining engine of a passing truck or the white noise of a distant highway.

It is no accident that the Psalms, which are the devotional heart of Scripture, were written as songs. Music heals. Music carries words to their destination in an irreducible and powerful way. At its best, speech has a musicality of phrasing and intonation that rhetoricians recognize to be fully as important as the "content" of what may be said. The retrieval of the Psalms as song in Taizé worship, or in the Gelineau Psalms, or in the musical settings we find in hymn books reminds us that to "sing unto the Lord" is a commandment for a reason. The words call us to attention. The music deepens that attention into prayer.

——————

Friday: Listen courageously

There are always things we don't want to hear. We protect ourselves from hearing more than we want to know. More than we can handle. More than we have time or inclination or courage to respond to. It takes courage to listen, for instance, to constructive criticism. Or an argument that threatens our favorite opinions. Or information that might require a change of habit.

I've encountered this resistance in conversations about food systems. Once you've read *Fast Food Nation* (Eric Schlosser) or *Eating Animals* (Jonathan Foer) or *Diet for a New America* (John Robbins), you can't be quite as comfortable in the supermarket. You look at labels. You try to bypass factory-farmed animal products and find there are no real alternatives. You wonder if you'll ever eat bacon again. "It's hard to want to know these things," a friend said, just yesterday, in the middle of Michael Pollan's *In Defense of Food*. "I have to reconsider some of my favorite foods. I wonder how much I'm willing to know."

She did finish the book, and now she's making new decisions based on new knowledge. I admire her for this. As I read more about the global problems we all face, I realize that practical ethics begin with challenging questions. "What am I willing to know?" "What points of view am I willing to listen to?" "What am I willing to do when new information threatens my own comfort zone?"

"Listen," Jesus begins, as he embarks on a teaching tale. "Listen! A sower went out to sow." "Listen to what the unjust judge says." Like a coach telling his team to "listen up," Jesus' word is a "heads-up." What you're about to hear requires close attention. What's coming will not be what you expect—you're in for a surprise. It may demand something of you. Listen, he seems to be saying, if you dare.

One of Mary Oliver's finest phrases comes at the end of "Morning Poem": ". . . whether or not/you have ever dared to pray." It's a line that surprises us into recognizing that prayer is a risky business, fraught with unforeseeable consequences. The same may be said of the willingness to listen and hear. Imagine really hearing the story of a fourteen-year-old who spends sixteen-hour days at a sewing machine on lower-than-subsistence pay to make the T-shirts we buy for $5.99. Imagine looking at labels with a more critical eye and passing up products that support slave labor. Imagine really listening to the stories of those with no access to health care, and taking on a new level of responsibility for the welfare of the whole community to which we belong and on which we depend. Imagine listening with open ears and an open heart for the word of life that silences self-interest and summons us to change.

Saturday: Listen when you pray

In Luke we read, "A voice came from the cloud, saying, 'This is my Son, whom I have chosen; listen to him.'" Remarkably, in this rare and dramatic moment of direct address, God does not say "worship him" or even "follow him," but simply "listen to him."

Mother Teresa offered a wonderful reminder of this insight in her answer to a reporter who asked, "What do you say to God when you pray?" "I listen," she replied. The reporter, unsatisfied, persisted: "Then what does God say to you?" She replied, "He listens." Active and practical in her ministry to the poorest of the poor, this remarkable woman didn't, apparently, besiege God with the urgencies of their many special cases, but spent her precious hours of prayer simply listening. Indeed, the simplicity of that listening lay not only in forfeiting particular agendas, but in forfeiting even the expectation that God had any instructions for the day, or answers to practical problems, or admonishments or affirmations.

In a life contemplatively lived, listening isn't exclusively a matter of waiting for God to speak, but of waiting *on* God—dwelling like a faithful handmaid in the presence of the One who calls us by name in holy silence.

The listening that is prayer starts not from the ears, or even from the mind, but from a heart open to recognize and receive God's voice in any of the many ways God may choose to speak. It doesn't anticipate particular answers to particular questions, though those may come, but trusts that what comes will be an answer. Sometimes that may be admonition. Peter heard it in the crow of a rooster, and repented. Pilate heard it in the courageous silence of a tortured man, and was troubled. Naaman heard it in the advice of a slave girl, and overcame the prejudices that were preventing his healing.

Carried into the occupations of the day, prayerful listening may enable us to hear God's voice in any number of unlikely places—in the neighbor's daily news update, the child's badly timed question, the interruptive phone call. Or in the silence of a solitary hour that comes as an occasion to be still and hear the voice of the Beloved, who comes "leaping over the mountains, bounding over the hills" to find us.

Receive

. . . the gift that's offered

. . . what you need for now

. . . the challenge you didn't choose

. . . teaching where you find it

. . . like a child

. . . forgiveness

. . . as graciously as you give

Sunday: Receive the gift that's offered

I'm not fond of birthday lists. Though there is value in asking for what we want, the "giftness" of a gift seems diminished when it's ordered up. A gift, freely given, says, "I thought about you, about what might please you, about what you might not get for yourself, about what might surprise you into trying something new." But it's hard to maintain a gift culture in a consumer culture where everything from cleaning products to churches is marketed on the basis of personal preference.

One of the few places we retain a sense of pure gift is in receiving what small children offer us. Our hearts melt a little at their shy, proud words: "I made this for you." No matter how crooked the ashtray (and how long it's been since you knew anyone who smoked) or how undecipherable the drawing, we receive such gifts as acts of unsullied love, and they delight us.

Occasionally we receive gifts we really don't like. They go into a drawer to be quietly retired or perhaps "regifted," on the dubious assumption that someone else might like them. Sometimes, before we discard an unwanted gift, it might be wise to see in it an opportunity for understanding the giver and for considering more closely something we didn't choose.

We get gifts that we didn't choose all the time. We get fog on a morning we hoped for sun. We get an invitation to a party we'd rather not attend. We get free tickets to a ball game when we'd rather go to a play.

Sometimes, of course, the stakes are higher. When we

are given a child with a health problem or responsibility for a parent with dementia, when we are laid off or projects run aground, it's hard to retain the sense that every circumstance may bear some gift if we are willing to receive it. The only way I know to be honestly willing to receive hard things as gifts from God is to consider how they foster the fruits of the Spirit: love, joy, peace, patience, kindness, goodness, faithfulness, gentleness, and self-control.

Even the best gifts may come with an unexpected cost. Every gift changes something—the shape of the day, the balance of a relationship, or just the space available on a shelf or in a drawer. To receive it is to accept that shift, slight or dramatic, and to make an adjustment.

When Jesus gathered with the disciples after the Resurrection, he conferred on them a gift that changed them and the course of history when he "breathed on them and said to them, 'Receive the Holy Spirit.'" It wasn't what they were expecting. Nor, when the Spirit comes to us, with inspiration or direction or unexpected comfort, are we fully prepared. But we can practice the open-heartedness that says "Yes—thank you—I accept," whatever it may cost, knowing the gift, yet to be fully disclosed, holds more promise than we imagine.

———

Monday: Receive what you need for now

In a recent workshop, I was asked to write a "memoir" consisting of just six words. I wrote, "Eat the manna.

More will come." It's taken me a long time to believe that. There were months in my childhood when meat was an unaffordable luxury, and the decision to go to a movie required a budget review. Confidence that "there will be more" competed with an abiding sense of scarcity.

But I learned from a resilient and faithful mother that manna still falls, and there *will* be more. She could tell story after story about provision that came just when it was needed. A donor's check appeared the same day an unpayable bill came due at the mission school. Someone arrived at our house with garden vegetables just when she wondered how she would stretch the groceries to make a few more real meals before payday.

Occasionally I had to overcome my adolescent irritation at her cheerful confidence in the face of my perfectly reasonable anxiety. Only after my own experiences of unexpected provision did I begin to develop a trust that could stop "taking thought for the morrow" long enough to receive gratefully what was needed for the moment.

A frequently forgotten part of the story of manna is that on the evening before it fell, a profusion of quail came to the Israelites' camp so the wanderers could have meat; the manna arrived after there had *already* been miraculous provision. Then, in the morning, "there was on the face of the wilderness a fine, flake-like thing, fine as frost on the ground." It's hard not to imagine this "bread" as something like the life-giving "lembas" of Tolkien's elves. This food was both sufficient and strange—so strange that its very name means "What is it?"

But the story isn't just about God's inventive provision. It's also about the discipline of taking only what you need. "Whoever gathered much," we read, "had nothing left over, and whoever gathered little had no lack." Whoever saved it overnight, against Moses' strict instructions, found that it was worm-ridden and foul-smelling in the morning. How clear can a teaching tale be? It's almost as though the closing line, curiously omitted, might have been, "Do you get it now?"

Still, let's not be glib about the realities of human need. We know that many don't get what they need. Every day, more than 25,000 people on the planet die of starvation or thirst. A naïve, literal reading of the manna story would lead us to a theological dead-end, since the facts don't seem to bear out its promise. Yet stories still emerge from the poorest parts of the world that affirm how God intervenes, provides, accompanies, and upholds those in the direst need in ways we can't begin to fathom.

Surely, in our abundance, we can afford to learn from those who live by faith at the outer edge of necessity. Even there they can receive with gratitude what they need for the moment, with no further assurance than that the One who provides remains with them on the journey.

———

Tuesday: Receive the challenge you didn't choose

Here's a bit of glib advice: "Look for the silver lining." And here's another bit that goes beyond glib: "Perhaps the cancer—or the accident, or the loss, or the disillusionment—is a gift in disguise." These are good things *never* to say to people in hard circumstances. We shouldn't try to assuage their pain with abstractions.

Still, there is truth in the idea that challenges, wounds, losses, disappointments, and reversals may sequester blessing. When we are the ones living through the hard moments, when we have taken the blow and felt the pain and grieved for a time, we can begin to open a space in our aching hearts for reflection on whatever blessing may be offered in the darkness. These blessings tend to be of several kinds: new wisdom, deepened compassion, fiercer faith.

To receive these blessings, we need only consent. The most powerful moment of prayer in my life came to me in a period when I was as close to despair as I've ever been. It came from a depth I didn't know I could reach; I remember that place when I read the psalm that begins, "Out of the depths I cry to you." But I didn't cry out; I thought I had no will to pray left in me. Then the simple sentence came, clear and kind and insistent: "Just say yes." So I did. Out loud. I just said yes. And then, like a spring in a desert, laughter bubbled up from the dry places in me. If anyone had told me that such a simple response would be all it took to restore hope, I would have regarded them as insufferably glib, perhaps even unfeeling. But since it came from the indwelling Spirit who speaks to us in our own dark and quiet places, I could receive it, and let it soften my hardened heart and redirect me from death to life.

I still don't think it's my place—or anyone's place—to

tell a person in pain to look for the gift in suffering. But if we tell our stories, we can encourage one another to remember that it can and does happen. Often.

~

Wednesday: Receive teaching where you find it

"Perhaps she's your teacher," someone annoyingly said to me once when I complained about a child's bad moods and worse behavior. "Perhaps she's teaching you about patience. Or boundaries. Or needs that you're not recognizing." These were words of counsel I didn't particularly want to hear. But when I began to consider them with a slightly more open heart, I realized that this understanding of "teacher" can help me view difficult people with more generosity, interest, and humility.

Boring people can help me practice courtesy; invasive people can teach me about healthy boundaries; selfish people can teach me about the difference between generosity and capitulation. But there's a level of receiving what others have to teach that goes beyond variations on "putting up with." It requires a further stretch into humility to consider others' behavior not in terms of their effects, but in terms of their needs or motivations or points of view.

"We never know who is walking beside us, who is our spiritual teacher," writes Mary Rose O'Reilley, who left her own teaching life for a time to live at a monastery and care for sheep. "That one—who annoys you so—

pretend for a day that he's the one, your personal Obi Wan Kenobi."

That every person and circumstance presents an opportunity to learn is a truth to which I willingly subscribe. To live that truth, however, is a challenge. I have not yet become "a person upon whom nothing is lost," though I love the idea that one might become such a person. To receive what another person has to teach, I have to stop protecting my own cherished point of view, and sometimes even let my skin thicken where it's too thin. Most of us live by what Wallace Stevens called "supreme fictions"—the stories we tell ourselves about ourselves, fraught with self-interest, and carefully composed to airbrush out our complicity in what has hurt us, or the ways we have masked selfishness, or the ways we have sacrificed divine adventure for a sense of safety. So we need people who step into our lives and mirror what we can't see about ourselves, who can help us navigate our own ambiguities, and ultimately enable us to tell our stories in a richer and wiser way.

"Receive my words," the writer of Proverbs says to his son, "and treasure up my commandments." Those phrases come from a culture that regarded advice from an elder as a gift to be treasured. Not all advice is equally to be treasured, but to receive words of counsel, warning, or instruction as gifts and ponder them before we decide where to put them might make us more open to the possibility that we are entertaining angels, unaware.

23

Thursday: Receive like a child

One of the best things about Christmas with small children is their indiscriminate pleasure in wrapping paper and ribbon, sometimes to the point of forgetting altogether the large box of Legos underneath. Small children enjoy what is given, often on simple, joyful terms that take the giver by surprise. We come into more complicated understandings of exchange and value as we learn the culture's social contract: you get what you pay for; when you receive, give back in similar measure; justice precedes generosity. But little children, before they learn the finer points of fair exchange, just get happy with what is given. Every gift comes as a surprise. They turn it over, often ignore what they're "supposed" to recognize as its finest features, explore its possibilities, and improvise with it in unlikely and amusing ways.

Jesus' words to his disciples—"Truly, I say to you, whoever does not receive the kingdom of God like a child shall not enter it"—can be read a number of ways. Understand that the kingdom of God isn't something you can buy or earn, for instance. Or receive the gift God gives without questioning the timing or the terms. Or receive without anxiety, guilt, suspicion, or any of the other attitudes we can develop as we grow into a complex economy of exchange. One way to read it is to remember the happy child opening a gift: receive God's gifts of community, moments of epiphany, and unexpected provision in trust and openness of heart. Be willing to be surprised, accepting what is given as an opportunity to play with new

24

possibilities, rejoicing in what is given without fear of loss or change, or regret for what was not.

This kind of childlikeness is not as easy as it sounds. The habits of conditional approval, suspicion, and attachment to security run deep in most adults. We've all suffered disappointments, felt our needs weren't met, received gifts that turned out to be burdens. But the gifts of God are always invitations. They invite us to deeper trust, newness of life, larger understanding.

The admonition to receive like a child reminds us that wisdom, understanding, and relationship with God begin in the trust that enables pure delight. St. Augustine's theology comes to a particular point when he says simply, "The end of all things is delight." It is what we were born for, as the old catechism puts it—"to enjoy God forever." And what it requires of us is a willingness to receive first of all, and most of all, a love we can return, but can never barter.

Friday: Receive forgiveness

Every week one of the things that motivates me to go to church, even when the path along the river lures me in its direction, is the moment in the liturgy when the pastor says, "Friends, hear the good news: I declare to you, in the name of Jesus Christ, you are forgiven." Every week I need those words again—spiritually and psychologically.

Receiving forgiveness does not come all at once, and

does not always come easily. While there is great relief in hearing the words "I forgive you" or "You are forgiven," there is also the inner voice that says, "But you're still guilty." Or "I don't deserve forgiveness," or "I still wish I hadn't done that!"

Receiving forgiveness takes trust—that the one who forgives means it, and that the relationship one has strained or damaged can and will heal. It also takes intention—to make amends, to live in the present and release the past. When you're forgiven, you get a task: it's time to let the past go. Paul speaks of rejoicing in God through Jesus Christ "through whom we have now received reconciliation." The reconciliation has been accomplished. It is true that growing in grace and maturing in faith take time, but it is also true that what has been done for us is completely and perfectly done.

Growing up in an evangelical tradition where there was a strong emphasis on "receiving Jesus Christ as my Lord and Savior," I came to feel that "being saved" depended heavily on me and my decisions. So I was startled when a friend told a story about a man who, being asked when he was "saved," replied simply, "The day Jesus was nailed to the cross." Not the day he decided to respond. Yes, the receiving completes the gift, but it is a free gift, and that "free" may be the hardest part of the Gospel to fathom.

The most necessary prayers we pray are "Yes" and "Thank you." They're good prayers for every day, morning and evening, no matter how short the shrift we give devotional time. "Yes" and "thank you" bring us back into alignment. They're like the breaths we receive and release: yes, I accept the gift of life and infinite love and endless mercy. Thank you. Now I can retrieve my energies from the sinkhole of guilt and turn them to the tasks at hand.

———

Saturday: Receive as graciously as you give

A lot of women I know (not to exclude men, but it has been my observation that this is especially true of women) have learned to be "givers." They take care of everyone at the party, they bring the extra dish at Thanksgiving, they go the extra mile for the fundraiser or the food bank. Bless them. But the giving habit, like any good thing, can go awry when it becomes compulsive. Giving can be a way of maintaining control or making sure that whoever is keeping score has assigned you extra points. There's the rub. Giving without grace is hardly a virtue.

Giving is a powerful and important spiritual practice. "Give something away every day" is a simple but profound exercise in acknowledging our common membership in the human community and in the fellowship of the Spirit. It's a reminder that what's "mine" is only really mine for a season, that life itself is temporary, that, as one wise woman put it, "It's all God's stuff."

Perhaps a good spiritual practice for habitual givers would be to be more deliberate about receiving—thinking of oneself each day as a recipient, stepping into that role with gratitude and trust, allowing others the pleasure of giving, along with the credit and thanks that come with it. The practice might begin by receiving the day as a gift, making gratitude for this day "which the Lord has made" a morning prayer.

To go through the day recognizing small gifts when they come—an opened door, a message of encouragement, an extra hug, an offer to take out the trash—is the beginning of a practice of gratitude that can reframe the particulars of ordinary life as a series of gifts that cascade quietly into our lives, often unacknowledged because they become routine. To recognize oneself as a recipient can be a vigorous act of reframing for one who has thought of herself as a "giver."

And what if, for a week, we were to practice saying "Yes! Thank you!" instead of "Oh, no, I'll do it. Thanks anyway" or "Oh, it's no bother. . . ." Allowing others to be generous toward us, if that isn't our first impulse, fortifies humility; we do depend on the generosity of those who love us, and on "the kindness of strangers." To be more intentional about that dependence is to deepen our awareness of the interdependence that strengthens communities where the free exchange of gifts is essential to spiritual survival.

The lovely line in John 1:16 is worth posting on the refrigerator or over the desk as a visible reminder of our situation as recipients, part of whose spiritual growth depends on living into that role with a healthy, life-giving practice of gratitude: "And from his fullness we have all received grace upon grace." "Grace upon grace" evokes an image of a waterfall, or of a garden with layers of color, or a corner where provisions for the poor multiply as full bags are quietly left, one by one.

There is no question about the wisdom of Jesus' saying that it is more blessed to give than to receive. But receiving graciously can also "bless him that gives and him that takes," and in its own way open hearts and hands in shared blessing.

Enjoy

. . . the moment

. . . the process

. . . the company you encounter

. . . the body you live in

. . . others' gifts

. . . those you were given to love

. . . the long journey

Sunday: Enjoy the moment

I recently saw a yellow road sign at the entrance to a rural meditation center that read "YIELD to the present." It's a good piece of advice.

Every wisdom tradition teaches the value of living fully in the present, not being anxious about plans or results, not squandering energy on fruitless remorse or pointless nostalgia. The moment is what we have. It's all we're given. By practicing "nowness" we ready ourselves for an eternity that, though we may imagine it as duration, has been described more mysteriously as absolute Now.

In his rich, contemplative *Four Quartets*, T. S. Eliot concludes a long, slow reflection on time with the words "And all is always now." Deceptively simple, the line offers a kaleidoscopic view of time: each turn of the kaleidoscope reveals a whole design, new each moment, all the same pieces revealed in a new way. And the last design is gone.

Enjoying the moment is easier and more meaningful if its pleasures aren't compared or measured. Sometimes the apparently meaningless tautology "It is what it is" can serve as a useful reminder that the satisfactions of this moment are unique, unrepeatable, and worthy of notice in and of themselves—not, first of all, as reminders or preparations or continuations, but as a constellation of small surprises that summon us to awareness.

Galway Kinnell's curious little poem "Prayer" offers a helpful way to pray for the grace to enjoy the moment:

Whatever happens. Whatever
what is is is what
I want. Only that. But that.

The "whatever" here betokens not indifference, but an intentional and practiced trust in the givenness of the moment, and a willingness to align one's own will with that of the giver. The want it expresses is not simple: I want the fullness of time—the fullness of this time, in all its abundant possibility.

Monday: Enjoy the process

The bottom line is not the point. Breaking the tape at the finish line, glazing the pot, bowing to applause after the performance, sending in the final draft—these moments of completion certainly have their rewards. But they are arguably no greater than the pleasures afforded along the way. Hikers know this. The tiny wildflowers that survive above the tree line, the sudden outlooks where the road bends and trees part, the sound of water over rocks, sitting on one of those rocks to rest—all these small pleasures provide their own answers to the question "Why go to this effort?"

I've been reminded more than once by people I consider wise that if your work doesn't feel, at least sometimes, like play, you're doing the wrong work. For one who is playing, the effort is its own reward. I remember the deep calm and delight of hitting a tennis ball against a backboard, alone in the schoolyard, again and again, feeling how my whole body was involved in each stroke, enjoying the particular thwack on the sweet spot. I remember a friend for whom making pots was a daily act of spiritual renewal, and meeting a master carpenter who touched the woods in his workshop with a tenderness most reserve for pets or children.

I vividly remember the way my mother visited the flowers and fruits and little succulents in her garden, pruning here, watering there, putting grateful hands in fresh dirt, and noticing new blossoms. She gave most of the figs and grapefruit away, made jam of the grapes, and bouquets for neighbors. Most of her satisfaction came from witnessing and sharing in the lives of her quiet plants.

It's a little too simple to say that process matters more than product, though often it does. To attend closely to process—to learn the appropriate skills, acquire the right equipment, and give our complete attention—is to open a hospitable space in which the Spirit can work. Then our work becomes a partnership with the One who moves in mysterious ways in us and around us.

When I was in graduate school, I posted a line on the library wall that helped me through many hours of reading, writing, and revising: "Attention—deep, sustained, undeviating—is in itself an experience of a very high order." These words came from a musician about whom I knew nothing—Roberto Gerhard. He certainly didn't know when he said them how they would transform one young woman's hours in the gray basement of a university library.

We can never take the full measure of the effects or outcomes of our work. Our business is to engage in the processes of learning, making, restoring, healing, negotiating, protecting, teaching, or even aging as wholeheartedly as we can. The results are in God's hands. The process is our calling.

———

Tuesday: Enjoy the company you encounter

"If you can't be with the one you love, love the one you're with." This widely quoted line from Stephen Stills' 1970 hit song can be read in several ways, some more redemptive than others. I like the line for its reminder to accept what is given—say, the person seated next to me at a dinner party where I was hoping to visit with someone else—as an opportunity. The one ahead of us in the grocery line, or next to us on the plane (where we hoped for the luxury of an unoccupied row), the new hire we didn't help choose, the business partner, in-law, or stepsibling visited upon us by others' choices—all get their bit parts in our unfolding stories. We get what we get, and we don't always get to choose; the art of living well and adventurously has as much to do with how we handle the relationships we didn't choose as how we handle those we did.

Several years ago a friend and I taught an experimental course we wryly entitled "Conversational English for Native Speakers." The purpose of the course was "to cultivate the kinds of verbal and social skills that make conversation an effective means of fostering good relationship, learning and mutual understanding, as well as a high form of pleasure." We asked students to read Jane Austen for vigor and Tom Stoppard for wit and Deborah Tannen for insight. In our semester-long conversation, a point arose repeatedly that I hope stayed with them: that thoughtful questions and genuine curiosity about another's point of view are life-giving ways to enter into any encounter.

Enjoying means exercising one's capacity for joy. I think of the exuberance with which Sherlock Holmes, in the old Basil Rathbone movies, would burst into a room, look around, spot an apparently inconsequential object, and seize upon it, exclaiming, "Hello! What's this?" His genius lay not only in his capacity for noticing but in his readiness to be interested, informed, animated, even waylaid by whatever came to hand.

At my father's funeral, the most moving observation my brother made was how readily and easily Dad would fall into conversation with anyone—a CEO or a store clerk or the night janitor in the school across the street. "He enjoyed people" seems a bland cliché, but in fact it is high praise insofar as it describes an attitude of willingness to engage with those who cross one's path in the hope and expectation that there is, as the Quakers say, "that of God in them."

The company we encounter may not be the company we keep. The patient we see for seven minutes in the clinic, the student we know for a semester, our son's high school sweetheart may not be with us for a long stretch of the journey. But if we consent to enjoy them, we may find, when they have moved on, that something of that joy lingers, like the scent of jasmine, as we go on our way.

———

Wednesday: Enjoy the body you live in

A recent survey revealed that 97 percent of women have at least one "I hate my body" moment in the course of a day. Dissatisfaction with one's body isn't restricted to women, either. We live in a culture in which bodies are commodified, marketed, and idealized, and unless we're very resistant, that involves us in a struggle to meet unrealistic and unhealthy standards.

Among the people I've met who accept and enjoy the bodies they inhabit are disabled, aging, and very young people. Acceptance may sound like a bland and boring virtue, but it is actually a rich discipline, arrived at only by way of humility and honest reflection. I think of a student I had years ago who could breathe only with the help of an oxygen tube, could not leave her wheelchair, and spoke with an effort. Her delight in the literature we read together was infectious, and her frequent laughter surprising. She had, no doubt, dark times. But it seemed clear to me and all who knew her that some source of peace and acceptance that extended well beyond resignation fueled her efforts to do work playfully in the world that she loved, despite the exceptional effort it took to navigate that world in the body she got.

I also think of a beloved mentor who celebrated her eightieth birthday by pushing back furniture and inviting guests to do the Charleston. And of a small child who, burdened with an awkward leg brace just as she was learning to walk, thumped along with great delight, unembarrassed and apparently undisturbed by what looked like a cumbersome and tedious slowness in her trips around the room.

These three people—among many others—gave me moments of humbling gratitude for mobility, however long it lasts. And gratitude for the amazingly versatile capacities we all have—the backup systems of brain and body that are more radically adaptive than most of us fully realize.

Care of the body is a calling; we are stewards of the bodies we're given. Sometimes care means correction of bad habits—say, gluttony, lust, and sloth, to name a few so common as to have made the list of "seven deadly sins." But care also means giving ourselves the kind of loving attention we give to others whose well-being depends partly on us. We need to rejoice in every kind of strength, beauty, agility, and intelligence we embody, and in the pleasures we receive when we swim, dance, stretch, hug, stroll, or simply stand at a window and witness a world that comes to us through the body's great gift of sight— and of larger vision.

Thursday: Enjoy others' gifts

Let us give thanks for Baryshnikov and Itzhak Perlman. For Rembrandt and Rothko. For William Faulkner and Toni Morrison and Maggie Smith and Renee Fleming. And for Garrison Keillor and Gary Larsen. That's not hard. Most of could make a long list of the people whose gifts we gladly celebrate.

It may be a little harder to celebrate those whose gifts seem to overshadow ours and to reduce our own significance in the communities whose good opinion we hope to enjoy. The one who was elected when we ran for office. The one who received the award we had some hope of winning. The one whose cooking is always praised, though our pastries seem just as flaky and our seasonings just as subtle. You know—those people. Envy is insidious, and it enters the most intimate spaces without warning.

I think the opposite of envy is celebration. I learned this from a remarkable woman who, despite many forfeitures in her own life due to illness and injury, brought a particular gift of appreciation into every encounter. I knew her well enough to know she had unfulfilled ambitions, frustrations, and even serious abuse in her distant past that prevented her from developing her own gifts in ways she had hoped. She had a brilliant mind, and might have been an attorney or a highly successful entrepreneur. She wrote beautifully and might have been a novelist of note. But the obstacles in her path meant that she spent a good deal of her time in bed, or moving slowly and with some pain, often depending on others to get her to appointments where painful treatments awaited her. These things were hard, and she acknowledged her disappointments: there was no false cheer about her. And yet she was cheerful.

Somehow she drew good cheer from witnessing others' successes and good fortune. Her genuine pleasure in a friend's promotion or publication announcement or opportunity for travel was an amazing testimony to that deep dimension of love that says, "Your happiness is my happiness. When it goes well with you, it is well with me." To call it vicarious pleasure is to diminish the radiant immediacy of her pleasure at others' good news.

I say these things not simply to eulogize this remarkable woman, who recently died, but to suggest that her gift of appreciation is one any of us might cultivate. There's real pleasure to be found in others' gifts, pleasure that may increase the more we meditate on the truth another friend insisted on: "There's no competition in the Kingdom of Heaven." What we bring, we bring, and all gifts are welcome at the great Wedding Feast.

In light of that, we can afford to appreciate. Every good gift adds to the great general good, which we are in no position to measure, except to be sure that even the smallest gifts, like the widow's mite, may be bigger than we know.

Friday: Enjoy those you were given to love

Yes. Those people. The ones who came by birth or marriage, the ones who arrived unbidden and stayed. The ones who seem to be part of our assignment.

Family and "family values" are the unfortunate subjects of much sentimental drivel—and the sometimes darker subjects that can drive us to seek therapy. Anyone who has spent time in counseling for depression or other forms of spiritual distress knows that family dramas are not always happy, and are often sites of pain and pathologies so entrenched we can barely trace their origins. Sometimes it's just as well not to retrace those entangled paths.

But family also gives us occasions for gratitude and growth. One of the gifts of awakened, aware adulthood is the capacity to cast a look around at those we were given and make new decisions about how to continue relationships with them that are healthy, gracious, and free. As a friend once put it, "When you get to be an adult, it's time to rewrite the social contract with your family."

For some this may mean taking more distance for a time so old wounds can heal. For others it may mean coming in closer and reclaiming and renewing precious friendships with those we've taken for granted. It's a good exercise to consider carefully and specifically what we are given and what we hope for in relationship to each person we were assigned by birth or marriage. Unlike the friends we choose, these are those to whom we are somehow obliged and from whom we must somehow learn simply because they're on the "mattering map" like features of the landscape. We may avoid them or even seek to escape them, but we "have" them, and it may be that our best option is to enjoy them.

The charming small children among them are no problem. Neither are the amusing storytellers and the generous makers of meals and the gifted listeners and the patient teachers and the ones who sat beside our beds with chicken soup. Enjoying the intimacies of caring and being cared for is one of life's chief delights.

Some of the lesser delights may be found in the eccentric uncle, the awkward adolescent with a phone in his hand and a chip on his shoulder, the narcissistic sister who really should get the counseling we're getting instead, the parent who doesn't quite understand that we're grown up. Enjoying them may be more of a project. It may mean looking a little more closely at anger to recognize it as pain, or listening a little more deliberately to tedious stories to hear the hopeful offer of a waiting heart behind the words.

And, of course, for the really hard cases—those who abused their power or the privilege of membership in the family circle for selfish purposes—enjoyment may be too strong a term. For those, the will and grace to forgive may be what to pray for. But when that prayer is granted, even there, there is joy to be found where none might have seemed possible.

Saturday: Enjoy the long journey

I've made several road trips across the country, and enjoyed them—mostly. There were moments when I'd seen one cornfield too many, and moments when I wondered why I hadn't, after all, decided to fly over Texas. Enjoying the long journey we're on—whether it's being married or raising children or working at a particular institution or persisting at a project that will take years—requires reminders of why we started it and reflection on why we're staying in it.

There's no particular virtue in "staying the course" just to say we did so. Sometimes a change of direction is a calling. Some journeys need to be reconsidered midway. Some are interrupted by illness, natural disaster, or loss. But the grand journey—life itself—continues. We don't have the whole map, though we have a guide. We don't get to plan the whole thing. We'll get lost along the way and need to be found. But joy may be available even in the lostness. We may discover new resources, new strength, friends we didn't know were nearby. Our assignment is to consent to what is given and seek the joy in it.

I love the moment in Tolkien's *Fellowship of the Ring* when Frodo, a small hobbit, untutored in the ways of warfare, consents to a daunting mission he never asked for: "I will take the ring, though I do not know the way." His words challenge me to accept, as discerningly and wholeheartedly as I can, the new assignments that come as the journey continues.

Frodo doesn't go alone; his companions, especially the

faithful Sam, see him through with wisdom and friendship and skills he lacks. Though his way takes him through troubles and terrors and even tedium, what there is to enjoy, he enjoys. He's grateful for rest, food, hospitality, good conversation, song, and pipes to smoke on the occasional quiet evening. He enjoys the grandeur of the Great Ones he encounters, and their kindness. He enjoys the gifts of lesser creatures not like him—the sprightliness of the elves, the doggedness of the dwarves, the cheer of Tom Bombadil, the reassuring power of Gandalf. He enjoys the journey because it is so clearly his; its givenness makes it not only tolerable but rich with a sense of calling.

Enjoyment is a gift and a skill and a commitment. Finding joy along the way means staying alert and receptive to opportunities for laughter and kindness and surprise even in rough territory. J. T. Barbarese's little poem about joy on the journey offers a memorable image of how joy invades the open heart:

JOY

sometimes shows up where nothing was
the way wildflowers will
suddenly be where nothing was
on the banks of highway hills

for some over-the-road truck driver,
who happens to sort of half-look
past the angles of his fingernails
down the cover of the matchbook

45

between his teeth, then asks himself
What's up with that old field
and feels his lonely surprised heart
shaken, and maybe healed.

Let Go

... *of self-defeating stories*

... *of yesterday's injuries*

... *of the side of the pool*

... *of the result*

... *of those whose paths lead elsewhere*

... *of one good so another can come*

... *when it's time*

Sunday: Let go of self-defeating stories

The stories we tell ourselves about ourselves are generally rooted in messages we received as children about our roles in the family (You're the wild one), our gifts (You're the math whiz), our gender (You're not very ladylike), or our character (You're the one we can count on). Much of the work that therapists and pastoral counselors do is to help people revise and reframe those stories. Our internal narratives often become self-fulfilling prophecies. "I'm a failure," "I'm a klutz," "I'm not very smart"—these become barriers to respecting and acting on our own ideas, to developing new skills, or even to receiving grace.

One of the many purposes of reading Scripture is to wander among its stories of human confusion, loss, discovery, and triumph and see in all of them how the Spirit of God broods over the waters, how God speaks in dreams, calls the unlikeliest people, and sends angels in disguise. It seems to me that one of the primary purposes of these sacred texts is to offer us stories to live by, not only to provide moral guidance but to complicate our oversimplified notions about success and failure, holiness and sinfulness, virtue and vice.

Scripture reminds us repeatedly that we are, none of us, in a position to judge ourselves any more than we're in a position to judge others. We make the moral decisions required of us with the best guidance available—or sometimes we betray ourselves and others and do what we know is wrong. But even those betrayals may open a back door somewhere for the Spirit to enter and renew us with an invigorating forgiveness that plants seeds of change.

I have loved reading biographies ever since I was old enough to enjoy Bible stories and the long shelf of "American Lives" books on the school library cart. King David failed spectacularly and often in the course of a turbulent life whose passions included avid devotion to the Lord and profound repentance for deep sins. Peter made a fair number of consequential mistakes on his way to becoming one of God's most powerful instruments. Abraham Lincoln endured not only hardships but also the torment of costly ambivalence as he took responsibility for the bloodiest war in U.S. history. Thomas Jefferson contributed arguably more than anyone in his generation to establishing an equitable rule of law, but he also owned slaves.

The best lives are riddled with ambiguities and lined with shadows. Each of them is a story about grace. To tell our own stories as stories about grace rather than stories about success or failure is to tell them more truly. That truth can set us free.

***

Monday: Let go of yesterday's injuries

Forgiveness can happen in a liberating instant of complete release, but for most of us it's a gradual—sometimes very long—process. Truly to let go of the injuries and insults we've suffered—a colleague's thoughtless disregard, a spouse's failure to appreciate our efforts, the undeserved anger of a parent or child—can take much longer than we might imagine. Traumatic injury or abuse can remain lodged for years in painful memories triggered again and again by small events that set off a chain of visceral recall. It would be immensely helpful if every abuse were followed by an appropriate apology and commensurate reparation, but that's not what happens. Some who inflict injury are unconscious of having done so. Some know that they've hurt you but don't care, or glibly assume what's past is past. (It isn't. Effects linger.) Some are so wrapped up in their own injuries that they can't bear to assume blame, and to protect themselves, they project it elsewhere.

So letting go is usually much more complicated than a neat transaction of confession, forgiveness, and absolution that brings closure and restoration. That's why letting go for the sake of one's own health and spiritual freedom—despite another's unrepentance—is so important. It is an act of self-liberation that demands a rare degree of clarity about how justice, grace, and freedom may be given.

Of course, letting go of old injuries isn't entirely a matter of the will. We can't just make ourselves "let it go." Sometimes forgiveness has to come without effort because effort doesn't get us there. I remember a vivid moment in my own life when my sense of hurt and anger toward a person who had hurt me suddenly lifted like a cloud dispersing. I had prayed to be able to forgive, tried to forgive, tried to imagine what it might feel like to fully forgive, but I hadn't gotten there. Then one day, when he was ill and I sat nearby, I discovered that the deep resentment I had borne like a pebble in my shoe was suddenly gone. I wasn't set free by a sentimental moment of pity. I was released from my pain in an amazing instant that brought with it an opening of my heart that felt like throwing windows wide to let in spring air. I began to understand his story in terms of his own pain, and discovered in myself an authentic curiosity about it that came to me as a gift of compassion I couldn't have manufactured.

So it may be a little too brusquely imperative to say "let go" of old injuries. But to ask for that moment, prepare for it, and expect it, is, I believe, to insure that at some point we will be surprised by joy and be free at last.

———

Tuesday: Let go of the side of the pool

I remember the feel of the rounded wet cement. I clung to it as I eyed the deep end, sure that I would sink like a stone if I let go. This climactic moment of apprehension may be avoided if one enrolls in the infant swim lessons now offered at most YMCAs and swim clubs. But I didn't receive that timely instruction and, at six or seven, doubted what my own eyes told me: that people with bodies bigger and heavier than mine could stay afloat.

I kept clinging for a while—long enough to bore my parents, waiting to cheer, and the brother who was trying to teach me—and then I let go. And my head went under. But I bobbed back up, and what I thought would be one brief shining moment—possibly my last—turned into an astonishing sense of ease as I dogpaddled further and further from the safety of the poolside.

I think of that sensation often; it has become one of my private parables, a handy memory in times of uncertainty or anxiety when the prospect of "drowning" or "getting in over my head" looms again. The side of the pool is always temptingly there. I know—I've spent days and years clinging to rituals of security that amount mostly to distractions from my own deepest purposes. I've showed up at social events that were safe and routine, carried out institutional obligations that were no longer life-giving for anyone, and clung to money when risking it might have offered significant education in generosity and trust.

And it's not just me. As we go along, we all weigh the difference between risk and prudence, adventure and security, the cost of suffering others' displeasure and the cost of avoiding it. It's a good exercise—that weighing. There's a time for prudence, and a time to consider security, and a time to forfeit one's own desires for another's sake. But my concern here is those times when we recognize a call to real risk or to a decision whose outcome we can't predict.

I faced those decisions when I felt called to give up a secure and satisfying full-time position to move across the country and begin something new. And when, for the sake of trying out a new path, I left a work environment where I was happy and respected for one where I was paid less and known only by a few. They were momentous decisions for me, but once I released my grip on the safe and the familiar, they were oddly easy—as easy as letting go of the side of the pool. Each time I discovered again that I could float. Something—someone—bore me up and would not let me go.

—

Wednesday: Let go of the result

Years ago I signed up for tennis lessons with a golden-haired beach-bum tennis coach whose unorthodox approach to the game amused and inspired me. One of his instructions went like this: Once you've hit the ball, you're no longer in control of where it goes. Let it go. Finish your swing with your whole body. Feel the pleasure of completion. Let the ball go where it's going, and relax into the yogic moment.

I'm not sure I ever fully "relaxed into the yogic moment," but the instruction stayed with me: once you've done what you can, let go of the result. There will be a result, but it's no longer yours to control.

A life in teaching has taught me this. Despite the efforts of accreditation boards to "assess" every learning event, one cannot see the real results of a semester's work. Students who test well may forget what the ones who went out with a C- will remember. Years from now, a line from *King Lear* or a stanza from an Eliot poem will come to mind when they need it—a bit of "equipment for living" they might not have had but for some classroom conversation. Teachers like me can hope for those results and delight in them when we hear about them, but we can't plan them.

It's the same with raising children. We pour our best love and efforts into them and give them to God. And it's the same with our health, our professional lives, our friendships—none of them, thank God, lies wholly within our control.

Every wisdom tradition teaches some version of this: Let go of the result. Take no thought for the morrow. Dwell in the present. Pray with open hands, open heart, open mind. God's rewards sideline "the bottom line." They come more often than not in ways we can't calculate.

And this truth brings to mind one of the paradoxes that snares us in a capitalist culture: though we don't want friends we would describe as "calculating," our dominant economic and business models aggressively encourage us to be exactly that. Consider those lilies—what might their price point be if we grew a hundred acres of them? And the birds of the air—well, let's be realistic: we can't limit our development plans to save their habitats. . . .

The appropriate alternative to that crass kind of calculation isn't sentimentality or naïvete, but a commitment to trusting that if we enter our tasks with focused, prayerful intention, doing the best we can to enable the results we hope for, we can leave it to God to correct our intentions and make our efforts fruitful, even when the fruits may be very different from what we expected—and even if they're brought about by what looks like failure. It's good not to judge too quickly what is a success. Stories about loss and failure, given a little time and perspective, turn out, remarkably often, to be stories about grace.

———

Thursday: Let go of those whose paths lead elsewhere

"Stay in touch!" we call as old friends pull out of the driveway, headed home to other cities, other states. And we hope to. We expect to, because we have so many technological ways to reach out. And as those ways have proliferated, we've lost touch with the real necessity of letting people go their way. "Good-bye" ("God be by you") was once a much weightier word than it is now; it signaled partings that were often permanent in this life, or at least long silences when letters traveled slowly and postal service was uncertain.

I think we all hope for the kind of friend who surprised my mother with an anniversary card a few years ago. She and my mother were both in their eighties. It wasn't my mother's wedding anniversary, just some random day in June. She opened the card to find the message, written in a slightly shaky but familiar script: "Seventy-five years ago today you first took my warty little hand and led me to Sunday school."

The woman with the warty little hand was someone I grew up calling Auntie Sue. She and my mother were still laughing together until a few months before Sue died. Deep friendships are immense gifts. Some of them last for a season. Some of them last for seventy-five years. But they all end. They are gifts to nurture and cherish, but not to cling to unduly.

Sometimes what we're called to do, even before death demands it, is to let go. The message to the disciples in the Gospels to leave home and go out into the world, to let the dead bury their dead—even the message to young people to leave father and mother—have a certain harsh clarity to them. If we've really consented to follow where the Spirit leads, we have to be willing to be led away from those whose paths lie in another direction.

It is not finally to a particular condition of life or institution or career that we are called to be faithful, but to the God who knows us and made us and is moving with us toward a place that has been prepared.

$\sim$

Friday: Let go of one good so another can come

C. S. Lewis's *Perelandra* is a fantasy story about the space travel of a mad scientist, Weston, and philologist Elwin Ransom, who secretly hopes to thwart his nefarious plans. They arrive on a planet where the Fall that occurred in Eden hasn't yet happened, and where a man and woman are living in a state of complete innocence. The woman they find there lives in trust that she's walking from one good to another. She can't understand why one would be reluctant to let go of one good for the next; it would be like clinging to one wave when you know another is coming.

Through this woman, Lewis explores what it might

mean to live in perfect alignment with divine will, accepting and accepted, untroubled by greed or envy or discontent. Even with his help, it's not an easy state of mind to imagine. We're taught to keep a firm grip on "the bird in the hand." Before they pronounce the benediction, Presbyterian pastors remind us to "hold onto what is good." Even the guys on "Car Talk" usually advised us to keep whatever car we have.

This is sound advice that serves us well—until it doesn't. Until it prevents us from receiving the next thing God has in store. There is a time, as Qoheleth would say, to hold on, and a time to open the hand, let the bird fly, and await what may already be waiting to alight. I have more than once left good and satisfying work on the supposition that other good and satisfying work awaited elsewhere and that God was, for reasons not altogether clear, calling. There were reasons to go—there are always reasons—as there were also reasons to stay. I have also undergone painful partings, some of which still tug at my memory and heart, to discover that, even as I mourned the loss, it made way for a new gift. Time and the heart opened in new ways. My attentions were summoned to new endeavors. Even after my more dubious decisions, life continued to be offered—and offered abundantly.

Since much of my work has entailed teaching undergraduates, I've had ample opportunity to see parents dropping off first-year students, weeping a little, lingering in the parking lot, loath to let go. In those moments the goodness of the going isn't too hard to affirm. The old metaphor of fledglings being pushed out of the nest still serves very well. As a hospice volunteer I've also had the privilege of watching families prepare for a final parting, each with its own mix of pain, dread, gratitude, resistance, and submission. Even these great losses leave room for the One who "makes all things new" to do a new thing.

The going and the coming may be laced with pain or fear, but each has its due time, that "fullness of time" in which things come to pass that are ordained but depend on our invitation. Our work is to say yes. And then say yes again, expectant and vigilant for the advent of what is even now being prepared.

Saturday: Let go when it's time

The final lines of Mary Oliver's sober and beautiful poem "In Blackwater Woods" remind us that living in this world requires that we learn to do three things:

> to love what is mortal;
> to hold it against your bones, knowing your life
>   depends on it;
> and, when the time comes to let it go,
> to let it go.

It's not always perfectly clear when "the time comes." Even the hour of death, given the options available now, often calls for ongoing discernment about when it's time to let go. Generally we can foresee the departure dates of children who are going off to college, or old friends who are moving, or young ones who are having babies. But when other changes loom and pend, the sense that "it's time" simply creeps up on us. That sense has little to do with clock or calendar; it presses at the edges of consciousness, and we become more and more uncomfortably (or perhaps gratefully) aware that the change to come is both imminent and necessary.

Sometimes the box of memorabilia you've loaded into four moving vans and stored in as many attics simply makes no sense to keep. Amazingly, the mice haven't gotten to it yet, or the moths, but its heft finally outweighs the purposes you thought it would serve. And the box of quilting squares, you suddenly know, will not become a quilt—not in your hands. Or your membership on a committee has gradually seemed more of a chore and less of a calling, and it's time to make a gracious exit. Or the work that you've loved is essentially done now, and it's time to retire. None of these decisions, small or large, is entirely simple, and none is in any way predictable. Knowing when it's time is a knowing that may come upon us like a sudden shower or like a slow dawn.

The wisdom of Ecclesiastes—that "to every thing there is a season and a time to every purpose under heaven"— offers assurance, and even guidance, but not explicit instruction. For that we have to rely on the Spirit, who meets us in the moment and breathes into us the deep breath of life that restores awareness, discernment, and decision. It seems to me most often true that those gifts of clarity, if they are of the Spirit, have a counterintuitive quality—something surprising, nonlogical, slightly unconventional—that leaves friends scratching their heads and asking, "Why now?"

Sometimes our sense of timing makes sense to everyone. But if we really want divine guidance, we may need to be willing to say "It's time to let go" in the face of all kinds of good reasons to hang on. Reason, as John Donne puts it, is God's "viceroy," but not the final arbiter of wise action. The fullness of time comes like waves do, obeying the laws of physics and gravity, but each one a unique event, called forth and performed with a breathtaking beauty and calm of its own.

Watch

. . . *for signs*

. . . *for teachers*

. . . *for surprises*

. . . *from a respectful distance*

. . . *and pray*

. . . *long enough to see*

. . . *through the night*

Sunday: Watch for signs

In his wacky 1966 novel, *The Crying of Lot 49*, Thomas Pynchon creates a world in which signs are everywhere, puzzling and cryptic and pregnant with impenetrable meaning. Once the protagonist realizes this, he begins to "read" his environment differently, and to find it replete with clues and directions. Though the novel is wild in its comic excesses, the idea of signs is not. Throughout both Testaments in Scripture, miracles, unusual events in the natural order, dreams, and encounters are identified as signs. In these many forms, God's self-revelation continues. The world is full of significance. Part of our spiritual work is to learn to recognize it.

Jonathan Edwards knew this: in *Images or Shadows of Divine Things* he inventories objects from the natural world—a river, a rose, hills and mountains, and so on—considering how each is a sign that imparts a message, a lesson, an invitation, a reminder of who the Creator is and how we are to understand and steward the created order. "The works of God are but a kind of voice or language of God to instruct intelligent beings in things pertaining to Himself," he writes. So, for instance, "The first puttings forth of the tree in order to fruit make a great show and are pleasant to the eye, but the fruit then is very small and tender. Afterwards, when there is less show, the fruit is increased. So it often is at first conversion. . . ." All the world, seen through Edwards's eyes, is a parade of messages.

Of course it's possible to over-read or misread signs;

our capacity for projection has been well documented by psychologists, and the artist Paul Klee has reminded us wisely and simply that "We don't see things the way they are. We see things the way we are." So we need interpretive communities to help us discern the signs that lead us toward personal decisions and the larger signs of the times.

Prophets are those who do this most reliably. They are the ones among us who look around and see what's unfolding and warn us. It may be given to any of us at any time to be the one to speak the prophetic word, which so often rests on a painful question: "Do you not see?" We don't. But we can learn to. We can learn to reflect on encounters, accidents, dreams, statistics, and the day's news with an eye for what forces are at work and where grace keeps happening.

God is making manifest all the time what we need to know. To watch for guidance is to live in expectation and trust that we are witnessed and accompanied and met and invited. All the time.

⁓

Monday: Watch for teachers

Teachers come when we're ready to learn. They show up in unlikely places. Sometimes they accompany us for a while as we move through a new season of life. Other times they offer us one lesson, and are gone. Of course I'm grateful for my primary teachers—for the good instructors I had in classrooms and for parents and grandparents who took their teaching function seriously. But I'm also grateful for friends who have offered correction with love; for strangers who spoke words I needed to hear, unaware of their sudden role in my life; and even (in retrospect) for difficult people who required that I open a door in my heart when I'd rather have kept it closed.

Some years ago I met a remarkable woman who by her own admission was raised in an abnormally protective environment. Her widowed father encouraged her to learn from books, but gave her very little experience of the world. She grew up and married a man who similarly kept her safe and ignorant in ways most modern women would find intolerable. Then, as it happened, both her father and her husband died, and she found herself in her thirties with no practical life skills—uncertain about how to balance a checkbook, plan a meal, care for her car, return an item to a store, or do her taxes.

"What did you do?" I asked her when she told me this story. "I decided I'd let everyone I encountered be my teacher," she replied. She asked her mechanic questions, and the people at the checkout counter, and bank tellers, and the people standing next to her in the movie line. She learned to take joy in learning. At the time I met her, she was driving a cement truck, having decided it would be a valuable skill.

Though her situation was unusual—even extreme—she taught me the value of assuming others have something to teach me, sometimes inadvertently, and keeping myself open to learning what they have to teach. Sometimes their teaching happens quite in spite of themselves: children teach far more than they can possibly realize.

Sometimes, too, a teacher appears at just the right time—the kind of teacher who may be the angel we are "entertaining, unaware." It's good, I think, to be on the watch for these teachers. In my experience, they show up and offer, but they rarely insist.

———

Tuesday: Watch for surprises

Wordsworth's beautiful phrase "surprised by joy," now perhaps just as widely recognized as the title of C. S. Lewis's autobiography, identifies with simple eloquence how God works in the world. Don Juel, writing about the Gospel of Mark, calls Jesus "the Master of Surprises"—a title that invites us to read the Gospel in terms of the many ways Jesus takes people, and continues to take us, by surprise. Not only the big surprises—say, raising people from the dead—but the moments of quick-witted riposte, the riddles, the sudden disappearances, the puzzling withdrawals and counterintuitive decisions, link him to the "tricksters" in folklore who bring wisdom in through the back door, or sometimes a side window.

I remember with particular fondness a friend who seemed always ready to be surprised. She seemed unusually attuned to the offbeat moments when an unexpected intrusion changed the shape of the day or the conversation, and she would pause over it to consider what might be beckoning. She had, as it were, one eye on the periphery to see who or what "showed up." An article on a newspaper's back page provided her with new material for a morning class—she had a lesson plan, but was prepared to change it. An interruption—even a rude one from a thoughtless student—proved to be an opportunity. Her willingness to be surprised modeled for me a species of hope: she received intrusions like quick passes from a teammate on a court, and she moved with them. Her agility was a delight.

If we're watching for surprises, we begin to recognize them—little offerings from a universe where there are more things at work than are dreamt of in the day's agenda. Gradually what may have seemed a mere interruption or an impediment takes on a look of possibility and promise. A child tugging at my sleeve may actually direct me toward something I might have missed. An untimely phone call—even the dreaded solicitation call—may remind me of a neglected intention to give a bit extra this month. A thank-you note may come at just the right moment to dispel a day's accumulated discouragements with reassurance beyond what the writer could have intended.

Watching for surprise almost guarantees that it will come, since surprise is the way of our Creator, who gave us a universe full of quantum leaps and subatomic particles that act like waves and inexplicable healings and epiphanic insights and prophetic dreams and curved space and breaching whales. The more we learn, as Einstein suggested, the more we know to expect the unexpected from a Spirit that "blows where it will."

Wednesday: Watch from a respectful distance

Susan Sontag's remarkable last book, *Regarding the Pain of Others*, raises the vexed question of when and how to witness others' pain. Focusing especially on war photography and the voyeuristic tendencies of a public with an appetite for violence, she asks whether our vastly expanded capability to record and disseminate images of suffering makes us more compassionate or less.

I remember a photo in the *Los Angeles Times* of a young widow on her knees, weeping at her husband's new grave. She lived in a combat zone where bombs could, and did, fall on civilians and military alike. Her visible sorrow was unlike anything I've yet been called on to experience. I was both compelled and troubled by the image. It was too close. I assume it was taken through a zoom lens, but it put the viewer into uncomfortably intimate space. The privacy of sorrow seemed to have been violated, perhaps in the hope of invoking sympathy, perhaps in the hope of getting a good shot onto the front page.

Space is a good gift. Especially living in urban settings, as most North Americans do, it's easy to bump into one too many people in the course of a day and end up in a state of general irritability, if not road rage. It's also easy to become a chronic spectator, curious not so much because we care as because we're idly fascinated by a couple's fight on the street corner, or by a neighbor's conversation about a local issue—because we know we disagree and plan to make her commentary into a story at the dinner table.

Richard Wilbur's poem "The Eye" begins by recalling an idle moment of spying through binoculars that happened to bring the neighbors into view, giving the speaker undue access. "What kept me goggling all that hour?" he asks himself, realizing he has, unintentionally, become a voyeur. The second part of the poem is a prayer to St. Lucy that begins, "Preserve us, Lucy,/From the eye's nonsense . . . ," and ends with a prayer for right seeing:

Let me be touched
By the alien hands of love forever,
That this eye not be folly's loophole
But giver of due regard.

Due regard is given from a respectful distance. It honors appropriate privacy and the solitude each of us needs at times to grieve or muse or rest awhile, free of obligation to respond to anyone but ourselves and God. Sometimes witness is best borne from a fair distance, or a phone call, away.

— ⁓ —

Thursday: Watch and pray

This two-edged imperative adds an important dimension to prayer. Vigilance as a habit of mind—noticing what's happening in the world around us, noticing where needs are, watching, witnessing and bearing witness—keep prayer specific and focused, like a healing laser beam trained on a tumor.

To pray well and faithfully is to pray attentively and expectantly, noticing where needs arise and noticing also how God might already be acting and answering. Praying for the sick includes watching for signs of change, noticing what's helping along the way and what isn't. Visits that might have been welcome at first might no longer be, as pain intensifies or fatigue takes over more hours of the day. Praying for a child who has behavioral problems includes watching enough to notice moments when something shifts and his heart opens, or he allows his fear to break the surface of his defensiveness. Praying for those in combat zones means watching the best news sources we can to understand what they may be suffering, to sharpen our compassion, and to bring them before God as real brothers and sisters whose suffering we have allowed to touch us.

I remember being horrified and moved by a news story about an Iraqi child who was killed in a bombing, and writing an elegy for him that began with what I knew of the facts:

He was nine.
His name was Ghaith.
His house was hit.
One piece of shrapnel
found its way
into his belly.

His father held him.
The clinics were closed.
All morning he bled.
They buried him in the garden. . . .

The event that turned into news that turned into a poem found its way into my prayers for some time. Ghaith's family is still out there somewhere, standing, in my imagination, for so many others who have lost children and who still mourn, unnoticed by a world that has moved on to the next day's news.

Watching as a dimension of prayer can mean seeing a thing through, even after the first shock has passed: the funeral was last month; the rape victim is back in school; the celebration is over, and thanksgiving may seem a mere echo, but it's good for it to go on, like the vibration of a Tibetan bell, into ordinary time. As we watch in the aftermath, practicing a lingering gratitude or a sustained supplication, we witness effects unfold for the grace that comes, new every morning.

Friday: Watch long enough to see

Watching takes time. What isn't quite so clear is that seeing takes time. "They have eyes and see not," Isaiah warns, speaking, it seems, about people who glance and look away, who skim surfaces, hunting for what confirms their expectations, who look only long enough to make the snap judgments or quick decisions that don't require wrestling with ambiguities.

In Maria Montessori's early years of professional life, during which she developed the theories of early childhood education that have served several generations so well, she spent many hours watching children at play. As she watched, she noticed more and more about what they did to educate and empower themselves, if left to themselves without undue judgment or restraint or even praise. She saw a child tie a bow fifty-three times before stopping, and realized the child had come to an inner sense of completion and competence no teacher could have predetermined. She saw how hungry children were for the learning that comes from touching, tasting, and experimenting, how delighted they were to practice simple processes like balancing building blocks, categorizing and sorting materials, preparing food.

As she watched, her respect for children's intelligence, curiosity, and sensitivity deepened, and she came to realize how much people miss when they underestimate children's wholeness, innate wisdom, and dignity. Her philosophy of teaching is rooted in that respect. Montessori teachers are trained to watch and notice and assist children in the work for which they're ready.

If we watched one another that way a little more often, we might see when someone needs permission to slow down and take a breath, when someone needs a word of encouragement she's hesitant to ask for, when it would lift someone's spirits just to be noticed. We might become more imaginative in our responses to those we're so used to seeing that we may be missing what's there to see.

—

Saturday: Watch through the night

Lately my sleep patterns have shifted. I drift off happily at bedtime, but now wake between three and four in the morning. I like to wake early, but not quite that early. At that hour, I'm faced with a decision: Do I get up and begin a day that will likely end in untimely fatigue, or lie there and try to find my way back to rest, if not sleep?

Nighttime is a time-honored metaphor for seasons of darkness, loss, uncertainty, mourning. It's not only a metaphor: nighttime is in fact when our demons tend to assail us, and unhappy memories or unnerving anxieties move to the foreground of consciousness, just before or after periods of restless sleep. It can be hard, in the dark, to maintain perspective and resilience. It can be hard, if we're tired, to appropriate those wakeful times for fruitful prayer or meditation. A fatigued mind isn't necessarily a relaxed one.

Wakeful nights, like periods of spiritual darkness, may be times to practice the kind of watching described in the story of Passover in Exodus 12: "It was a night of watching by the Lord." It was doubtless also a night of anxiety, restlessness, and hope mixed with apprehension and unknowing. But the Israelites knew the Lord was abroad and something was afoot, and so they watched and waited,

75

not only that night, but in ritual remembrance "kept . . . by all the people of Israel throughout their generations."

Since then, the night watch has become a part of Christian ritual, remembered liturgically in the Christmas and Easter vigils, and by the custom of watching with the dead the night before burial.

Sometimes it's good to remember how much germinates in the dark of our lives—like seeds in the darkness of the soil, or like trees fattening their leaf buds in winter. During those times we never know what's being prepared within us, because it hasn't yet broken into the light of consciousness. The Spirit works within us in ways we barely imagine, and can only—and only sometimes—recognize after the fact.

When we think we're simply thrashing about, wandering aimlessly in the fog, there may be, as Hamlet reminds us, a divinity shaping our ends.

Knowing that, we may submit to that process of being shaped and tried and prepared with a little more patience in the waiting and awareness of the subtle signs that come even in the very midst of darkness. They remind us of how the slow sun rises, as Emily Dickinson so beautifully and accurately put it, "a ribbon at a time." Those ribbons of light may be pale and thin, but each of them is a promise and a harbinger of far more to come.

Accept

. . . what you cannot change

. . . the terms of time

. . . the body's demands

. . . the open spaces left by loss

. . . even those you avoid

. . . your assignment

. . . the invitation

Sunday: Accept what you cannot change

Anyone familiar with twelve-step programs knows the serenity prayer, which asks for the serenity to accept what we cannot change, the courage to change the things we can, and the wisdom to know the difference. As often and as widely as it has been repeated, it has not been flattened into cliché because it is such a sturdy, serviceable prayer, anchored in real wisdom about what we need as we go our bumpy ways. Real acceptance is neither passive resignation nor simple capitulation, but active, imaginative, open-hearted reframing of what is given us to work with.

I've often found curious comfort in the little tautology "It is what it is." It seems a gentle way of relinquishing false hope and taking stock of facts. Once we have those facts clearly in front of us, we can work with them—reconsider, reframe, reorient ourselves.

A friend of mine with a mysterious chronic ailment that had remained undiagnosed for years appeared on my doorstep one day exuberant—not because she had found a cure, but because she had a diagnosis. She knew now that what she had was a rare form of a chronic illness that couldn't be cured but could be managed. She couldn't change the fact of the illness or the likelihood of the prognosis, but she did have a new sense of direction upon which to base her strategies of daily life. She knew her limits and accepted them as the boundaries within which she could exercise her considerable creative energies, budget her time, enjoy her friendships, and rest when she needed to. Letting go of false hope gave her real hope.

One way to think about hope is that it is a choice to receive what is given and remain open to its possibilities. Real hope depends on relinquishing false hope: it takes courage. A dear friend of mine longed to travel but struggled with back problems. After her eleventh back operation, she finally released the hope she had harbored right up until that final journey to the operating room. As she and I talked, she let go with one long sigh the itinerary that was to take her through the Alps and on to India. In the same conversation she began to invest her energies in what she *was* given—grandchildren who appeared on her doorstep with guitars and chewing gum and stories; an immigrant gardener who pruned her roses and repaid her generous interest with his genius for bringing life out of drought; an unfinished novel she decided to resurrect and write with the help of an adjustable bed and new laptop.

Those of us who can afford even these luxuries have sources of human hope many don't. One reason to travel by TV or others' stories to areas of the world where people live in unimaginable poverty is to witness their humbling endurance, which defeats despair, and their astonishing acceptance, which allows them to make the next meal of a small bit of rice or cornmeal and serve it with dignity. They teach us acceptance and humility even as they remind us to work more zealously to change what we can.

Monday: Accept the terms of time

Kodak's encouragements notwithstanding, we can't "capture the moment," though we certainly try. Picture-taking is more pervasive and promiscuous than ever, given the popularity of photo-snapping smartphones. While personal photos offer significant pleasure and contribute something vivid and valuable to our shared stories, they also contribute to a cultural delusion that most of us suffer from to some degree: that we can get those recorded moments back. But the simple truth is that we can't. And to the degree that our images divert our attention from the present, we're in danger of overlooking what the present moment has to offer.

I remember going to a school performance recently where the walls were lined with parents holding video cameras, phones, or other recording devices, their faces hidden behind lenses. All of them were jockeying for position to get a good shot, fiddling with the focus, and altogether oddly inattentive to what was happening onstage. My husband and I didn't take a camera, much to our daughter's dismay. We tried to explain to her that our intention was to be fully present to the performance, to take it in, enjoy it, and not focus on making a record of it. But our point was largely lost on her. The generation she's a part of has been increasingly conditioned to live life with a lens in hand, or in someone else's hand, a poor substitute for eye contact.

I'm not advocating a rigid asceticism with respect to our multiple means of mechanical reproduction, though

I do know people who have benefited from "electronic fasts" during Lent. What I am suggesting is that there's something to be gained from reflecting on how to live the lives we've been given in this dimension. It's important to live in time, receiving each moment as new—focused and full of its own possibilities—and to let it go when the next one arrives, taking no thought for the morrow, living in trust, and releasing ourselves from the past as we keep our energies and awareness in the present.

Clearly that doesn't mean forfeiting memory or story or even images of the past, but perhaps it does mean not allowing them to drag us into pits of nostalgia or lure us into mazes of anxiety. Accepting the terms of time is like accepting the way we need each breath, receiving and releasing life again and again, gift upon gift, grace upon grace.

Tuesday: Accept the body's demands

They say the poet William Carlos Williams slept only three hours a night during his long and rich double career as doctor and poet. They say the same about yogis, and about a number of highly visible CEOs whose profit margin may have some relationship to waking hours. Most of us, though, need sleep. And rest. And unstructured time and moderate exercise and nourishing food.

The notion that "the body never lies" is worth considering. Our bodies provide records of our wounds, our stresses, our nutrition, our exercise, our psychological history, the anxieties and enthusiasms we register and carry. And sometimes we must protect these bodies against the very culture that claims to support them. North American culture, for all its overwrought focus on health theories, offers every conceivable temptation to abuse the body by overindulgence.

Discerning what our bodies really need means resisting the tug of those temptations, paying attention to our bodies' messages—pain, fullness, stress patterns, food reactions—and respecting them. Of course, like a lot of "simple" advice, paying attention may not be so simple. When we make a habit of ignoring those messages, it takes will and effort—and sometimes a good support group—to learn to notice them again, the way young children do. In fact, this retraining period may be a good time to reflect on the richness of what it means to "become like a little child."

Care of the body is a stewardship practice. These bodies are the equipment we've been given for this earthly journey, and much of our spiritual as well as our physical well-being depends on our proper care of them. Perhaps less obviously, care of the body is a practice of humility. In a culture of competition and reward, it's easy to fall prey to the collective delusion that more stress and less sleep means our work is more important than that of people who keep saner hours. Or that sugar, alcohol, and saturated fats are a key to pleasure and some measure of "the good life." They're not.

It's time to redefine "the good life." We can start by

humbly accepting our own limits and physical needs, and educating ourselves about how best to meet those needs. It's one more way to remind ourselves of what it means to be human—breakable, vulnerable, limited, dependent, and yet beautifully, fearfully, and wonderfully made.

———

Wednesday: Accept the open spaces left by loss

Solitude and silence can be challenging, even scary, especially in the wake of significant loss. When a beloved person dies, the memories—of their daily habits, of their route around the house, of the voice we won't hear again—are haunting and painful.

Whatever gifts of new family and friends the years bring, loss leaves an empty space that can't be filled because no one can be replaced. It's tempting to fill up the time and fill in the gaps when grief threatens to overwhelm us. It may be that old movies and late-night phone calls are exactly what we need to keep us from the pit of depression or the cliff-edge of despair. But there are those times when the open hours or the empty chair face us with stark and unavoidable loss.

Accepting that emptiness, as challenging as it may be, can be a way of turning devastation into healing silence. Where the conversation has stopped, we may after a time begin to hear something else—inner promptings in new directions, thoughts that give birth to new ideas, the voice of the Spirit that prays within us.

Other losses may also become journeys of acceptance. Moving and leaving friends behind, seeing children off to college, losing a job—all these can be stressful and sad. I know more than one person for whom even a timely and welcome retirement has opened up empty, uncomfortable space in the day when it's easy to feel disoriented, unneeded, no longer useful.

Into that open space may come a new calling, if one waits with an open heart, and direction and purpose and life-giving occupation. Every season of life brings losses, which leave open spaces that may be best left open. We may recognize them as fallow periods when the soil restores itself for whatever may grow there as the season turns and a time for planting comes round again.

Thursday: Accept even those you avoid

Most of us could name a few people we'd just as soon not see again, but who continue to cross our paths. Sometimes avoiding people who give us grief or anxiety or make us grind our teeth with irritation or stifle yawns of leaden boredom is the better part of wisdom.

But it's worth considering what it might mean also to "accept" even those we don't like or choose. It may be that they were given to us chiefly for the purpose of learning to set good boundaries. Acceptance doesn't have to mean inviting them to lunch or enduring a painful hour in their company. It could mean learning to say no in liberating and generous ways to those who want to control us or own us or recruit us to serve their private agendas. It could mean praying for the kind of grace that helps both them and us grow a little in clarity and self-awareness.

Accepting the irritating officemate or a relative who presumes or a nosy neighbor (and here I invite you to make your own list) certainly doesn't have to mean much in the way of offering them our precious time. And it certainly ought not to mean maintaining insincere friendship. But it may mean that, from a safe distance, we take on the challenge of imagining what needs or fears or aches lie behind their offensive behaviors. That act of imagination can be an exercise in generosity. And generosity can be offered from safe and appropriate distances—in prayer, in small nods of encouragement, or simply in helping to preserve the space and time someone else may need. We can give whatever we can afford, which is something we need to determine with prayerful consideration. What we can't afford isn't ours to give.

Some of us, of course, have abusive people in our lives who need to be avoided for the sake of safety and sanity and peace of mind. To accept them doesn't require that we ever see them again, but it may mean being willing, since they found their way into our stories, to imagine and hope for and pray for their healing. To pray for their healing is a way of praying for our own. If we can accept even them as instruments of grace who teach us tough-loving, self-respecting wisdom, we may find our own way out of fear and, mysteriously, help them do the same.

Friday: Accept your assignment

Those of us old enough to remember the TV show "Mission: Impossible" will recall the line that occurred near the beginning of every episode as the spy got his orders: "Your mission, should you choose to accept it. . . ." What followed was a partial revelation of the dangerous and demanding task to be undertaken.

We don't get our assignments on earth in quite the same way, nor do we have quite the same degree of choice in the matter. But the idea that we're here on assignment, for a purpose, on a mission of sorts, is appealing to me. It also seems fairly clear that we don't know the whole of our own deepest purposes, and don't need to. We're called to walk in trust every step of the way.

That journey of trust begins—and continues—with acceptance. Consider the simple act of consciously, intentionally accepting every fact of the life you've been given. I accept the family I got. I accept the body I got. I accept the schools I got. I accept the place I was given to live in. I accept the moment in history I was born into, with all its complexities and possibilities, both frightening and exhilarating. I accept the gifts and challenges and tastes and opportunities that have equipped me and directed me to the path I'm on. I accept the losses, the disappointments, the false starts, and the mistakes I can choose to learn from. I accept my age and my aging, the friends I have, and the unsettling people who challenge me. I accept what is unresolved and uncertain, ambiguous and puzzling about my journey in this world.

Acceptance is powerful in the ways it can diffuse pointless, malingering guilt—both our own and that of those around us. Imagine how our simple acts of acceptance might free these people to say what they're actually feeling—or even to feel what they're actually feeling. There are certain kinds of truth we only recognize and tell in places where we feel accepted.

So maybe acceptance is the assignment: accept the terms of the life God gave you, accept what comes, accept the grace that comes with it, accept the limitations that are also the means by which you develop imagination and ingenuity and patience and humor and compassion. It's a large and exhilarating assignment, should you choose to accept it.

Saturday: Accept the invitation

"What does this writer invite me to do?" This is a question I suggest students ask themselves in courses where they're reading books that stretch them in new and sometimes unwelcome ways. To read books, poems, plays, or essays as invitations is to recognize that reading involves consent and collaboration. The writer may invite me to venture a little beyond my cultural comfort zone. She may invite me to entertain a point of view that I find alien, or to postpone the satisfactions of plot development in favor of slow, exquisite character portrayal.

Artists do the same thing. To imagine that Picasso or Mondrian or Rothko have a gift for us when what we've learned to love are Vermeer's women by windows or Michelangelo's well-defined David means accepting an invitation that is also a challenge: Come with me, and I'll show you how to see a new thing—but you'll have to leave your old expectations behind. You have to let go of something to get the gift. Want to come?

I believe this is what the Spirit does: invites us, again and again. Without compulsion, but by means of every small circumstance, we are invited to let go, step up, enter in, practice resistance, pause and discern, forgo, laugh, recognize abundance, reframe our expectations, say thank you.

When my daughter was in an improv class, she taught me (and made me practice) the exercise of just saying yes to whatever happened to happen onstage. If three turtles wander in from the wings, accept them and reframe things to include them in the scene. If someone screams, accept the cue to respond in a way that introduces new plot possibilities.

To accept in this sense does not mean to capitulate—quite the contrary. It means to take it on. To play with it. And in that moment of improvisation, to enter into a state of grace that says yes to the great Imaginer, who equips us with exactly what we need to respond to the call of the moment.

Resist

. . . the pull of power

. . . the seductions of the semi-annual sale

. . . the force of habit

. . . mindless media

. . . the comforting self-deception

. . . dithering and distraction

. . . the usual temptations—again

Sunday: Resist the pull of power

Empowerment is a strong motivator. Very shortly after they learn to say "Mama," children learn to say, "No!" and "Mine!" and a bit later to declare, as does one child I know and love, "I can do it mine-self!"

Psychologist Alfred Adler considered the drive toward personal power to be the basic human drive (unlike Freud, who believed it was sex, or Jung, who believed it was the spiritual drive toward wholeness). Regardless of which of those giants won the "basic drive" contest, the desire for power runs deep, and all our stories, all our family conflicts, all our wars are, among other things, about power—who wields it, how they got it and keep it, how different forms of power co-exist or threaten each other, how it's related to gender, class, race, and what becomes of the powerless.

In light of how pervasive power dynamics are, it's good to remember what Jesus had to say about power: "Blessed are the meek, for they shall inherit the earth" (Matt. 5:5). Also the peacemakers, and those who are persecuted for righteousness' sake. The spiritual condition that Jesus was teaching wasn't abject powerlessness or subjection or capitulation, of course; quite the opposite. Meekness and peacemaking of the sort he prescribed—which Quakers, Mennonites, and many others involved in peaceful resistance have modeled—take extraordinary courage, faith, and ingenuity.

We need only think of Martin Luther King's preaching truth to his political enemies, the scores of protesters who allow themselves to be arrested as they stand up for human rights, or of the young man who stopped a tank in Tiananmen Square by simply standing in front of it. What the world regards as power is limited and deceptive, and its rewards are temporary and fraught with anxiety. The rewards for humility are endless.

It's easy to understand the distinction between "power over" and "power to." The former is selfish, destructive, deceptive, and tempting. The latter is the capacity to carry out meaningful, generous, effective work in the world, and comes by consent and consistent effort to develop understanding and skill. Empowerment that enables us to act freely and confidently is worth claiming and advocating on behalf of those who have been rendered powerless by the radical inequities of the social and economic systems we inhabit.

Doing all we can to make sure the poor get a fair hearing in court means supporting those who do the strenuous, humble work of public defense. Making sure that girls have access to education in countries where women are still threatened by abusive policies means supporting those who speak out at great risk—like Malala Yousafzai, whose efforts on behalf of women's education won her the Nobel Prize, but only after serious threats to her life.

We may not find ourselves on the front line of social struggle, but we can always participate as back-up by donating, signing worthy petitions, and praying without ceasing until wars cease and the poor are fed. An assignment this large can only be undertaken by those who refuse to succumb to the temptations of personal power, and who seek the paradoxical empowerment that comes only through humility, commitment, collective action, and prayer.

Monday: Resist the seductions of the semi-annual sale

The semi-annual sale is only the tip of the iceberg. There are also the deftly-spun accessories ads and the urgings to update electronic devices and the slogans for which someone was paid a six-figure salary. We are a highly targeted market.

The forces at work on our willpower are enormous. Our tastes have been meticulously tracked, analyzed, and charted. Marketers study us with a close intensity that is evident in the personally tailored ads that appear on Facebook pages, the recommendations sent by Amazon that read like personal notes beginning with our name.

Judith Levine's entertaining book *Not Buying It: My Year without Shopping* recounts her efforts to forgo all but necessities for a year. It was a way of recalibrating the difference between want and need and resisting the market forces that drive us toward habits of consumption that are ruining both personal budgets and the planet's ecosystems. As Levine takes stock of the desire for stuff that has come to seem like an addiction, she recognizes a deeper desire arising out of the rubble of packaging and possessions:

I do want something that religions offer in abundance: the permission to desire wildly, to want the biggest stuff—communion, transcendence, joy, and a freedom that has nothing to do with a choice of checking accounts or E-Z access to anything.

Others have attempted similar experiments. The Internet is alive with blogs by people who advocate simple living for reasons of spiritual health and social justice. Take Bill McKibben's little book *Hundred Dollar Holiday: The Case for a More Joyful Christmas*. Here McKibben reflects on what values may be retrieved by believers who are intentional about resisting the rampant commercialization of our holiest celebrations. The "buy nothing" project and buynothingnew.org are similar efforts to encourage practices of simplicity and frugality not only for economic reasons but because our deepest human values are at stake—justice, love of neighbor, peace.

McKibben tells a story about the TV program "Teletubbies," whose spin-off products are aimed at "filling the one-to-two-year-old niche" in the market. When even our babies are a target market, and armies of young professionals are taking careful aim, it's time to recognize that there's something lurking in big-box stores that's worth resisting.

Tuesday: Resist the force of habit

Habit is powerful—and healthy, up to a point. It saves a great deal of energy that would otherwise go into dozens of small decisions a day. Since I don't have to decide which side of the bed to sleep on, or where to put the mail, or what to eat for weekday breakfast, I can spend the energy I would have put into those deliberations elsewhere. And habit can be the foundation of a virtuous life: habits are the exercises that strengthen us in love, joy, peace, patience, courage, justice, temperance, and fortitude.

But habit can also make us blind to possibilities and opportunities. It becomes a track, and then a groove, and sometimes a deep ditch. Since occasions of grace often arise quietly, in a by-the-way sort of fashion, we might miss them when they lie just outside that groove.

It's easy to fall into habits of discontent and frequent small complaints, especially if our complaints become a source of general amusement and a way of engaging the people around us. It's easy to fall into habits of sloth. When we decide some of the small things that keep life orderly and peaceful don't matter, more and more things may be added to that list, until general squalor and disease become the new norm. It's easy to fall into habitual postponement of good intentions (I'd like to volunteer—maybe next week) or habits of distraction (social media come to mind) or habitual erosive practices in daily living that remain unexamined—short-circuiting intimate time with those we love, sacrificing courtesy for convenience, skipping quiet time to move on with morning tasks.

The force of habit is strong, and it strengthens as time goes on. Resisting it requires intention. Deep intention—focusing mind, heart, will, and desire on the good you seek—reinforced by conversation, companionship, and prayer—is stronger still. It may be that the way to resist erosive habits is to set our hearts on a way of life that involves the play of the Spirit and prepares us for surprise.

To remember when we wake that "God laughs and plays," as the Christian mystic Meister Eckhart wrote, might help us venture out of our grooves and ditches and follow the gentle guidance of the Spirit, who comes to us "new every morning."

Wednesday: Resist mindless media

Even those of us who mock its mindlessness—most of us—resort to the odd sitcom or talk show when a demanding day has exhausted our energy for loftier things. "Chilling out" in front of the TV can offer legitimate pleasure, sometimes education, and sometimes inspiration—to cook like the Iron Chef, or to try out a new talent like Paul Potts, or to change our eating habits after hearing a TED talk about sugar. Mindful media do exist.

The mindless media are the shows that work like narcotics. What to me have seemed the most reliable measure of value in books, films, and TV are two questions: "What does it invite me to do?" and "What does it require of me?"

If I'm invited to cheap amusement, uncritical acceptance of what I know is morally questionable, if my tolerance for violence keeps rising and my appetite for sensationalistic news keeps growing, it's a good bet that the downward tug of those spurious pleasures needs to be resisted. If I'm not required to think as I watch or read, to pause and reflect, consider and weigh possibilities, heighten my self-awareness as I notice my own responses, if I'm not required to wrestle with a certain amount of ambiguity, paradox, or complexity, that book or film or show is probably a waste of time.

The appeal of mindless entertainment is that mindfulness is strenuous and sometimes painful. Thoreau writes about the "higher life" we "fell asleep from," and suggests that most of us are at least half-asleep a good part of the time. He concludes his long reflection on the examined life with the claim "Only that day dawns to which we are awake," meaning that we only get the full value and gift of time we fully and mindfully inhabit.

We probably can't live mindfully without each other's help. There need to be those with whom we sustain lively conversation, play games, hunt for interesting rocks on the beach, listen for birdcalls in the woods, read aloud. There need to be those with whom we are comfortable in restorative quiet and whose presence quiets our restlessness. We need to offer those gifts to the people around us. And, now and then, snuggle down in front of a really good movie.

Thursday: Resist the comforting self-deception

I continue to find it surprising when a person I think of as discerning and thoughtful greets a piece of compelling evidence with the oddly irrational insistence "I just don't want to think that's true." I've heard that line in response to a grisly description of the conditions in factory farms ("I don't want to know—I just want to eat my meat!") and to descriptions of political corruption ("I just don't want to think people who go into public service would be so cynical") and to observations about the implications of climate change ("Well, I imagine they'll find a way to reverse it before our grandchildren grow up").

I don't exempt myself from this population of occasional deniers and hiders from the truth. I imagine that all of us sometimes befriend the most available bearer of false comfort at times; they're easy enough to find. Many of them are making money from what they purvey. But what we want to think may lead us dangerously astray from what we need to be thinking about.

None of us has the whole truth, of course. Whole truth belongs only to God. We may have sufficient evidence for an informed opinion, but the bottom line on any significant question recedes into mystery. Still, there are things we ought and need to know because our lives, communities, children's welfare, compassion, and deepest, truest comfort depend on seeking and consenting to know what truth we can. We need to be willing to look and understand and consider the implications of hard truths and hard facts that we'd rather not know in order to prepare ourselves to respond with resilience, intelligence, and kindness. If I remain in denial about a child's alcoholism or a spouse's depression or the effects of fast food on a family's health, I may be contributing to risk.

Barbara Ehrenreich's provocative book *Bright-Sided,* which explores the dangers of "positive thinking," makes a valuable point: if we train ourselves to always look on the bright side, we may never contribute meaningfully to solving problems that develop in the dark. Positive thinking isn't the same as hope. It bears the same relationship to hope that the false comforts of Job's "friends" bore to the challenging message of God, whose only comfort was to answer "why" with "who," and to invite Job to live into the mystery of relationship with divinity itself.

Friday: Resist dithering and distraction

T. S. Eliot described modern people as "distracted from distraction by distraction." His phrase comes to mind on days when immediacies disrupt my clearest intentions for the day, and small, unplanned incidents distract me even from those. Buddhists speak of "monkey mind" in describing the way our thoughts can leap from one image, memory, anxiety, or plan to another, causing us to lose the focus and calm from which our best decisions are made. The Internet, for all its enormous advantages, hasn't helped us maintain focus. "Hypertext" and its offspring and offshoots invite us down every rabbit trail that Google can map, so the five-minute Facebook session often turns into forty-five minutes.

"Dithering" was my grandmother's word for what I do when I start down those trails. When I was a child, I spent many hours in her cheerful, pious, and elegant company, and I learned how many small habits had moral consequence. She taught me (with a great gentleness and good humor that made the lessons palatable) to recognize that the small things were the big things in disguise. Not that all occupations had to be equally serious. But dithering wasted time that might be spent more deeply and truly enjoying even the frivolities. Whatsoever your hand leadeth you to on the bookshelf, she might have said, read it with your whole attention.

W. H. Auden writes about that quality of attention in "Sext" from his canonical hours, where he observes how easy it is to tell if someone is following a real vocation: it is the beautiful "eye-on-the-object" look. I remember recognizing that look in the fiercely trained eyes of Björn Borg, the legendary tennis player, and in the deep concentration of Vermeer's "Lacemaker," and in the focused gaze of a calligrapher drawing a word with such beauty and care that it took me right to the opening verse of John's Gospel. That, Auden understood, is what vocation looks like. Or devotion. Or fidelity. Or the self-forgetting kindness that pays complete attention to the person we encounter, perhaps by chance, perhaps by divine appointment.

If we look away too soon and dither on, we may be missing the treasure that sustained attention reveals, however ordinary the time or the task.

Saturday: Resist the usual temptations—again

To hear something described as "tempting" generally gives it an aura of the desirable. Chocolate cake is tempting—never so much as when one is trying to eat less fat and fewer calories. Watching a movie instead of preparing next week's report or grading papers is tempting. Gossip is tempting, especially when it can be masked as concern. Spending is tempting, especially when a want can so easily be rationalized as a need.

But the evils of today are probably a lot like those of yesterday, and will likely arise to tempt us again tomorrow. I'll crave that last bite of cake again, even though I know I won't feel better after eating it. I'll want to watch that Robert DeNiro movie, even as I dread the task that looms after it. I'll be eager to share the news about my next-door neighbor even though I know it will spread like wildfire. I'll feel compelled to buy the lovely sweater displayed in the store window, even though I have a drawerful of similar ones at home. Renewed temptation lies in wait for me—as it does for us all.

The good news is that, over time, we can train ourselves to be less tempted. A friend who developed adult-onset diabetes had to radically reduce his sugar intake. After six months he remarked that he finally realized how sweet an apple is, and, knowing that, was far less tempted by sugary treats. Necessity, for him, was the mother of delight. Like my friend, we can all substitute more acceptable temptations for those that are prurient or damaging to health, relationship, or well-being. We can resist temptation with the help of Weight Watchers or a nicotine patch or all manner of automated reminders on our iPhones.

But there's a reason the prayer Jesus recommended for daily use includes the line "Lead us not into temptation." Because it lurks. And not only trivial temptations (though these are often seriously erosive) but those that mask consequences we might fear to contemplate.

Habit is the basis of real virtue, some philosophers would tell us. But it is also the basis of vice. I'm likely to be tempted again today in exactly the same way I was yesterday. Knowing myself (which philosophers also recommend) has to include some moral inventory of those particular seductions and a clear intention to meet each of them with prayer, resolve, and the help of my friends.

That last point is important. One of the many reasons we thrive best in community is because we can help each other resist temptation. We're not all tempted by the same things, thank God. So when we need somebody to lean on, it's good to turn to those who find it easier to remind us why we should resist. Because we'll feel better. Because we'll be happier. Because we thrive best when we're in alignment with the generous will of the one who "doeth all things well."

Allow

. . . time for the unfolding

. . . space for the stretch

. . . things to emerge

. . . things to coalesce

. . . for a little slippage

. . . for emergencies

. . . for surprises

Sunday: Allow time for the unfolding

A good plot takes time. To do justice to any story of human development or discovery—falling in love, coming of age, suffering a crisis, recovering from loss—one has to allow time and space for the complications, ambiguities, and possibilities to unfold, for other points of view to be presented, for some setbacks to occur that recast the original purposes. A story is not a race to the finish line.

Nor is life, with all due respect to St. Paul's vigorous use of that metaphor. Life swirls and eddies, stalls and starts again, leaps and lingers and takes unanticipated detours that often turn out to be avenues of insight rather than simple inconveniences. To allow things the time they take is a practice of humility: hurry, Paul Tillich observed, is a violation of the gift of time.

Because post-industrial electronic culture assigns such high value to "efficiency" and speed, taking time is a challenge. Slowing down, letting insights or decisions take their own time, waiting for possibilities to germinate, allowing time for reflection—all these require countercultural resistance. Giving ourselves and each other permission to take a little extra time may be an important act of generosity that opens up breathing space in a day—and in a relationship. My pastor-husband knows better than I the wisdom of slowing down. One of the many kindnesses I receive from him is his frequent response when, in a rush to get out the door, I call, "I'll be right there." He says, "Take your time," and the moment changes. There's breathing space. "Only five minutes" becomes "Five whole minutes." A sense of abundance is restored.

Gardens teach us as vividly as anything in the world what it means to allow time for things to unfold. A rose going from bud to bloom, an apple changing from green to pink to red, yellow beans growing plump on the vine—the surprise is both slow and sudden. We watch from day to day, and one morning, in the fullness of time, we witness the completion.

We hear the phrases "in due time," "all in good time," "in God's good time," "when the time is ripe." Each of them invites reflection on the intricate biological, psychological, and spiritual processes and rhythms that sustain us, and reminds us to enter into those processes without haste or anxiety, trusting that time is a teacher, if we consent humbly to its terms. When we do so, we may find that right respect for time opens a door to the timeless moments where we may glimpse eternity.

―――

Monday: Allow space for the stretch

More and more of us live in urban settings. We huddle in elevators, bump shoulders in the subway, creep along in rush-hour traffic, work in cubicles, navigate crowded sidewalks, stand in line at the ATM. Wise city planners work hard to provide green spaces, because they know our physical and mental health depend on them. IKEA brings us design ideas for small rooms that give at least the illusion of spaciousness.

Spaciousness is more than a feature of architecture or outdoor life. Open spaces open the heart and imagination and spirit. Spaciousness is a spiritual state that can be renewed where limbs can stretch and the eye can see a far horizon imported into the smallest room. On a stay with a lovely English woman in her modest row house some years ago, I was about to set a bowl of potatoes on the only remaining space in her tiny kitchen when she stopped me. "Don't set it there, please," she requested, though the other crowded counter didn't offer much by way of alternative. Then she smiled, explaining, "I know there's not much space, but for that very reason, I need a bit of open space—one clean surface that makes me feel I'm not completely surrounded by clutter. It's a little discipline I keep." The inconvenience seemed an unreasonable price to pay at the time, as I carefully relocated other dishes to retrieve a bit of real estate for the potatoes. But her words stayed with me. "I need a bit of open space."

Growing up with the privilege of a home with a yard in a state where beaches and mountains lie within easy reach and wide vistas are not hard to find, I'm aware of the restorative, life-giving value of open spaces. So I appreciate the dedicated groups trying to preserve wilderness and beach access and urban parks for all of us. I appreciate architects who recognize the need for natural light and air in classrooms and hospitals, and even the makers of "tiny houses" who artfully maximize limited space. And I appreciate spiritual teachers and directors who understand, as Lacy Clark Ellman wrote recently, that "space is the foundation of a contemplative practice—space for silence, for stillness, for solitude; space for rest and for delight and play; space to wonder and ask questions; space for emotions to surface and for roots to grow deep."

In yoga and other forms of body work, the stretch is a key to opening the body as well as opening the mind and heart. We get stuck—literally and figuratively—and need to stretch, just as we need to eat and drink. The practice of spaciousness—the wide embrace, the deep, slow breath, the quiet hour, the patient listening—makes way for the Spirit to move and alight and dwell.

Tuesday: Allow things to emerge

Most of us can remember planting our first garden seeds when we were about five. And then, growing curious and impatient, trying to pull up baby carrots or radishes to see how they were doing. Doubtless some kind parent or teacher explained why it was important to leave them in the ground, thus delivering a life lesson we'd have to learn again and again. For some of us, the temptation doesn't go away—to lift the lid of the pot, ask more than our kids are ready to talk about, over-explain, over-plan, try to control the outcomes.

The title of Barry Stevens' cheerful little classic *Don't Push the River* has helped me long after I've forgotten most of her musings on Gestalt therapy. Her book's title reminds us how ridiculous it is to force processes that need to take their natural course. Pregnancy will take the months it requires. Children will learn to walk when they're ready. Love follows no one's calendar. Collective consciousness will reach critical mass. Political will comes to a tipping point. And though we may track how these things happen by survey or story or collecting data points, they're not entirely ours to control. Things emerge.

There's a simple Buddhist directive that applies here: "Don't strive. Allow." This small teaching, when I remember it, takes remarkable and immediate effect. Suddenly I can relax into the process, whatever it is. To remember that I don't have to make things happen—that solutions will surface, that the trajectories of mood and meteors will follow their course, that what has receded will return—I become observant rather than anxious. When I don't try to manage what's happening, I can become a witness.

The Latin word *mergere* means "to dip." "Emerge" suggests the return of something that has dipped out of sight or mind or reach. It will come forth in due time. The best teachers know this, as do parents. Children learn when they're ready. If we let it, education proceeds from epiphany to epiphany, and awareness emerges like the sun rising. Montessori's whole philosophy of early childhood education rests on this idea: the task of the teacher is to prepare an environment in which learning may happen when the moment is ripe. "Ripeness is all," Edgar reminds us in *King Lear*. And Hamlet famously observes that "There's a divinity that shapes our ends, rough-hew them how we will." Our efforts to control may in fact impede the emergence of what is truly needful.

One of my favorite stories about an answer to prayer is one that my husband told, gleeful and marveling, after a walk on the beach one day. Troubled by matters he couldn't resolve, he said to God, "This would be a good time for you to send me a sign." It wasn't necessarily an answer he needed so much as a little wave of reassurance from God that all would be well. As soon as he gave shape to the request, he saw, offshore, a gray whale slowly breaching. "It rose straight up," he reported, lifting his arms high above his head, "and it hovered there longer than seemed possible. Then it slowly sank and resumed its leisurely swim further out to sea." What we need is just under the surface, I was—and am—reminded. If we allow it, it will emerge.

~

Wednesday: Allow things to coalesce

I like watching where adjacent ripples of water come together, two systems of concentric circles intersecting and modifying each other. I like watching a roomful of women making contact before a workshop begins. I like learning about those moments in history when things came together instead of falling apart, and the center held.

"Coalesce" comes from Latin words meaning "nourish" or "grow up" preceded by the prefix "with." Imbedded in that word history is a reminder that it takes time and slow tending for disparate visions and agendas to converge, and for tensions to resolve into shared energy and direction. In physics, Wikipedia tells us, coalescence "can take place in many processes, ranging from meteorology to astrophysics. For example, it is seen in the formation of raindrops as well as planetary and star formation." Musicians and artists, fascinated by the idea of coalescence, have entitled their compositions, paintings, and rock bands "Coalescence." The title expresses an ideal and a hope.

The process of allowing things to coalesce differs fundamentally from corralling or controlling. Coalescence speaks of natural affinities, a movement toward meeting and merging that we recognize when people fall in love, when political groundswells become apparent, when families reconvene around a loss, recognizing a level of relationship that underlies the fissures and divergences of adult life. We gather, but in a deeper sense, we are gathered. Something draws us together for at least the one brief shining moment that reminds us we were put on the planet for a common purpose. And the calling continues.

The ecumenical vision is one of coalescence. If a divided church is to come together after centuries of theological opposition, it will surely be a result not only of the efforts and intentions of those who organize conferences and write books, but of the force that summons us all toward the final unity we proclaim when we sing "We are one in the Spirit," and pray "that our unity may one day be restored."

The movement toward the center is happening as

surely as entropy. What has scattered will be gathered, in due time. Maybe not in our lifetimes; we are here only for a short part of a long process. But to see history and our own lives in terms of a deep dynamic of coalescence is to recognize how "centering" godly work is, how "centering prayer" opens us to coalescence, and how much of our best participation may not be paddling madly, but floating on the currents that take us all home.

Thursday: Allow for a little slippage

Architects have to plan on slippage because houses settle. Financial advisors counsel investors to allow for some slippage in money management plans. Vehicle designers factor in a little clutch slippage, even though it reduces the transfer of engine power to wheels. And when you're building a sand castle with small children, you want to pack it pretty heavily because some of the sand is going to slip off.

Efforts to batten down every hatch and close every loophole generally result in rigidity, defensiveness, tense relationships, fear, and frightening fundamentalisms. Jesus seems to have had more harsh words for the legalistic enforcers of laws than he did for any other single group. His own moral instruction, delivered largely by way of parables, questions, and sometimes riddles, allowed ample room to grow into the wisdom toward which it invited his listeners, meeting them wherever they were in their spiritual development. The same words offered milk for the babes and meat for the fully grown, as Paul put it. Jesus allowed for the play of possibilities and a certain amount of imagination and inventiveness in interpretation. Poetry and wisdom texts always open spaces where associations and images can slip around a bit before they settle.

"Slippage" is a scary idea if predictability and control give you a sense of security. I've lived in earthquake country long enough to know that to hear the term "slippage" from a real-estate broker when gazing at a downslope can evoke apocalyptic anxieties. The best brokers, though—and we had one—can say the word with a note of carefree resignation that reminds a potential buyer that we all live with some form of uncertainty—in the earth, in the climate, in the money market, in our health.

Security is an elusive objective, and one that becomes dangerous when it trumps more generous concerns for each other's welfare and erodes the practice of trust. We certainly have ample historical evidence that security itself, isolated from greater values, can be a dubious and dangerous objective. Whether the circumstances are historical or personal, larger or smaller, it's always wise to allow for the possibility that things won't go according to plan, that they might go distressingly awry, and that "awry" might turn out to be what calls forth in us some capacity for ingenuity, invention, or adventure.

All of nature allows for slippage. Evolutionary process, the movement of soil, water, and tectonic plates, the uncertainties obstetrics has failed to eliminate, the mysterious stages of dying, the fate of fish eggs and polliwogs, the subtle forces that shape a child's development—all these are subject to unforeseeable circumstances. And that may be very good news. We don't get to control all outcomes—and we don't have to.

Friday: Allow for emergencies

Emergency preparedness is one of those practical tasks I need to be reminded of repeatedly. My husband and I have a box full of emergency rations and water somewhere in the garage; I think we've buried it under buckets and camping gear. We have flashlights, though I'm not sure they all have batteries. We even have pre-stocked daypacks full of emergency supplies recommended for the trunks of cars. But they're on a shelf somewhere.

I'm not proud of this. To acknowledge this ill-preparedness in print motivates me to focus more steadfastly on the days we have been warned about, when power failure, earthquake, fire, flood (or, in the parched land I inhabit, drought) disrupt our complacencies.

Allowing for emergencies means factoring them into our plans—knowing that all plans are contingent, that the day might bring a life-changing moment, and that the moment is what we have. Taking no thought for the morrow is one way of allowing for emergencies; the fewer plans we try to lock in, the more spaciously we live, allowing for what emerges, what "comes to light," as one etymological dictionary puts it.

To "take no thought for the morrow" in the biblical sense is not to be unprepared, but to know oneself to be prepared in ways beyond our conscious control: we will be given what we need when the time comes if we live our days in the practical trust that keeps us connected to the source of all resilience and ingenuity.

A little four-year-old of my acquaintance went through a difficult season of coming to terms with the unpredictable world in which he found himself. When things didn't go as he expected, he often wailed in dismay, "That was not in my plan!" I tried not to be too visibly amused, since his distress was quite real. But I did find myself smiling to recognize in him such a familiar, frank admission of the very human longing for an order and a control we can't have.

What we can have is a confidence that comes from training (in first aid, tire-changing, fire safety . . .), connection (to each other and to God), and a habit of mind that releases our anxieties into a great ocean of mercy that may terrify us from time to time, but bears us on its waves as we follow a course we didn't chart.

Saturday: Allow for surprises

Every once in a while, a student of mine who's never spoken in class, and who seems to have occupied his back-row seat with sullen reluctance, says something relevant and insightful. And I am surprised once again into recognizing that learning may be happening where I thought seed was falling on stony ground. Every once in a while, a hospice patient who has seemed depleted and exhausted will greet me with mystifying energy and clarity. And I am surprised once again into realizing how life ebbs and flows and how the Spirit moves even on the weakest breath. Every once in a while, one of the people I believe I know best does something "out of character," and I am surprised into remembering that we see each other "through a glass, darkly," and each of us is ultimately known only to God.

Preparing for surprise is something of a paradox, but like most paradoxes, there's wisdom in it. Not all surprises are happy ones, to be sure, but all surprises are teaching moments. What they teach us is humility and resilience, if we're able to receive the gift of surprise. To prepare for surprise is to remember even as we make our plans how much may change in the course of an hour, and to hold our plans lightly, with an open hand.

Surprises are occasions of grace. "All things," Annie Dillard writes, "live by a generous power and dance to a mighty tune." We are taken by surprise ("overtaken" is the original, literal meaning of the word) when that generous power moves us out of the small sphere of our own will and designs into a larger, more kaleidoscopic design that turns like the spinning globe even when we think we're standing still.

Surprises are often moments when, with a shock of

recognition, we become aware of what was there, just below the radar, all along. What takes us by surprise has been happening. Surprise is a meeting of consciousness and circumstance—not chance or coincidence, but part of something much larger. Now and then we see the larger pattern, but, being human, we "cannot bear very much reality," as Eliot reminds us.

Some babies seem to live in perpetual surprise at the strange new world they inhabit. Without preconceptions, they may see, more clearly than they ever will again, the colorful panorama of unsettling possibilities we are called to. We smile at their long, wide-eyed gaze. May they remind us to remain in a state of radical amazement that, even on the most mundane afternoon, allows for surprise.

Be Still

. . . before you act

. . . in the midst of the noise

. . . and watchful

. . . so you can hear the sound of life

. . . so the Spirit can move

. . . before you speak

. . . until you know

Sunday: Be still before you act

Several years ago, at a retreat on spiritual discernment, I received this piece of advice: If someone asks something of you, take a moment before you answer to check in with yourself and with the Holy Spirit for guidance. If the person is pressing you for an answer, stop and blow your nose. Or go to the bathroom. Do whatever you must to give yourself the space and time, even if it's momentary, that you need to make a clear, informed, prayerful decision.

At the time, I laughed over the homey practicality of the nose-blowing and the bathroom retreat, but the advice has proven its value. It's a version of the ancient advice to "make haste slowly."

Something happens in the pause. We retrieve a perspective that's easily lost under the pressure of someone else's expectations. We have a chance to ask ourselves a few questions that put the request into context: Is this really the call of the moment, or a distraction to be resisted? Am I about to say yes out of a need to please? Would my yes come from generosity rather than capitulation? My no from wise stewardship rather than selfishness or sloth? These are deep questions, and they generally deserve more time than it takes to pull out a handkerchief. But when we make them habitual, they act like a filter through which all decisions pass with fair efficiency.

Claiming a moment of stillness in the midst of decision-making is also a practice of the presence of God, a chance to remember that we stand in the presence of Love itself, bathed in it, upheld by it, embraced, forgiven, and, when we are willing, guided by it. When we stop the momentum, we regain balance and readiness the way a tennis player returns to the center after each shot to ready himself for the next.

I am old enough to remember Björn Borg's stillness on the courts at Wimbledon. He didn't dance around waiting for the next shot, but stood planted, still, his eye trained on his opponent, his body ready, but at rest, as though conserving every micron of energy for the next move. "Great athletes are lazy," a tennis coach laughingly told me once. "They don't waste a motion. They keep all their stored energy for the thing they want to spend it on."

I wouldn't say "lazy" was the perfect word choice, but I took his point: great athletes know when to be still and wait, and exactly when to move. So, I imagine, do great strategists of any stripe. And great saints.

—

Monday: Be still in the midst of the noise

You notice those people. The ones sitting at the long table who are listening rather than arguing, flirting, or holding forth. The ones who don't hurry to fill the silences in a conversation. Surrounded by chatter, they create an island of stillness around them that gives off a kind of radiance.

Good teachers do this: they stand in the midst of a noisy classroom and wait while children notice the stillness and quiet themselves. I've tried this myself. Often it works to bring the chatter in a room to a natural pause without my having to raise my voice. People notice quiet and respond to it. Stillness can be a powerful experience, both for the person who enters it with clarity of intention and for those in the force field it creates.

Each year retreat centers are filled with people seeking stillness. Everyone I've known who has ventured on a silent retreat—whether a day, a weekend, or five days without speaking—has found it a powerful, heart-opening experience, deeply restful and often illuminating. My own experience of such silence is that at first I become more than usually aware of ambient noises. Passing trucks, a gardener pruning tree branches, the clatter of pans in a distant kitchen, even birdsong may seem intrusive and distracting. But after a while, as the stillness deepens, the noise recedes, and silence begins to feel like a warm pool in which I am buoyed and bathed.

Prolonged silence throws into sharp relief the noise we have come to accept as normal. Never before have humans lived with the level and variety of ambient noises we tolerate now in urban life. Even the constant low hum of electrical devices—refrigerators, motors, air-conditioning units—contributes a measure of stress to mind and body.

Stillness is healing. A recurrent, intentional, prayerful practice of stillness, even brief periods of it in the midst of a noisy day, creates a refuge, a place to return to and rest in, and a habit of being whose delights are an open secret among those who are called to be bearers of quiet. If we are among them, we hear that quiet "in the deep heart's core," as Yeats put it, even while we stand "on the roadway, or on the pavements gray."

———

Tuesday: Be still and watchful

"Be still before the Lord and wait patiently for him," the Psalmist writes. In the Psalms and throughout Scripture, it is made clear that "wait" is an active verb. Faithful waiting is expectant, hopeful, focused, attentive, watchful.

"Be watchful," Paul advises the Corinthians, and later the Colossians. And Peter echoes his words: "Be sober-minded, be watchful. . . ." Waiting and watching train the mind and the senses and attune them to God's guiding presence.

I remember lying on a hillside by the Russian River one August night with my three daughters, all of us in sleeping bags. We were watching for shooting stars. It was the time of Perseid meteor showers—a thrilling spectacle for those willing to scan the skies with "soft vision," waiting patiently for the next sudden spitfire of light to arc across the darkness and disappear, leaving only its small, swift reminder of cosmic mysteries and the allurements of astrophysics. There were long gaps between sightings, during which we exchanged a few words and a little laughter, but mostly we lay in companionable quiet, watching and waiting.

There was an art to the watching. If we fixed our gaze in one spot, we were likely to miss an event in some other corner of the skyscape. But if we scanned back and forth too quickly, we might miss what was too sudden to catch on the fly. So we learned to let our eyes rove slowly, achieving a kind of visual directionlessness, like the slow drift of water in a pool, following an intuitive path. I was reminded of the lines in T. S. Eliot's *Four Quartets*: "I said to my soul, be still . . . and wait without thought/for you are not ready for thought." Something just below the surface of thought—feeling, hope, receptivity, primal awareness—awakens in this kind of waiting, and is watchful in the way of animals, alert to dangers and possibilities, but not exactly afraid.

Some of our watchfulness is rooted in habits of fear. But those habits can be healed by the deep, reassuring, patient love of God given by someone who knows us and sees our needs. Such love can train us in new habits of quiet anticipation. The watchfulness that is full of love rather than fear seeks to protect what is sacred, prepare for what is promised, and be ready always for divine surprise, which sometimes, like the fog, comes "on little cat feet."

Wednesday: Be still so you can hear the sound of life

Everywhere life is happening—in shopping malls and classrooms, at mills and factories, at dinner tables. Also in those quiet, wild places where the most conspicuous sound is the wind. And in intensive care units where the whoosh of the ventilator offers a poignant reminder of how all our breath comes and goes as we receive life and release it again and again. Behind every sound there is a story.

The truck driver gets up early, leaves his love to sleep, pours coffee into a thermos, and climbs into the cab at first light. Between crackly dispatches, he lets his mind wander. He knows his route too well to have to think about it. The wild turkeys just down the road are in a flap over the garden snake dangling from their brother's beak. Their covetous squawks last about a minute; then they return, each to his or her own foraging. The raucous laughter of students shuffling to the bus stop, backpacks laden, covers the myriad anxieties of the young—the self-critical voices, the shameful secrets, the romantic hopes that grow among small disappointments. The barking dogs have resumed their task of protecting the humans in their care. And something small that scurries under the azalea bush too quickly to see is finding its daily caterpillar.

In his poem "And I Said to My Soul, Be Loud," Christian Wiman writes these bold and whimsical words: "I am the sound the sun would make/if the sun could make a sound/and the gasp of rot/stabbed from the compost's lumpen living death/is me." In a similar spirit of deep, playful awe, Mary Oliver has claimed that when she sits quietly in open spaces, "I can hear the almost unhearable sound of roses singing."

With the Psalmist who wrote, "Let all that has life and breath praise the Lord," we might listen to all those sounds—subtle and strident, natural and mechanical, human and animal—as a chorus of life and a convergence of stories that may now and then gather into a song of cacophonous praise.

<hr />

Thursday: Be still so the Spirit can move

If we really want the Spirit to work in our lives, we have to stop grabbing the controls and trying to do everything ourselves. When our interior spaces are filled with plans, anxieties, curiosities, even the morning's news or good intentions, we leave little room for the Spirit to enter. The Spirit of the Lord may "blow where it will," but the force of that mighty wind may be diminished by the obstacles we put in its path. The Spirit may blow us over, but most often, it seems to me, it weaves its way quietly, courteously, and subtly through the scattered minutes of an ordinary day.

"God is subtle," Einstein claimed, and one of his biographers adopted that rich yet simple claim as a title: *Subtle Is the Lord.* What is subtle is not likely to be noticed except in relative stillness. Unless we stop the inner chatter and screen out distractions, we miss promptings and guidance that come subtly—in a fleeting expression on a familiar face, in a nagging thought at the edge of memory, in a pattern of "insignificant" events that emerges, over time, into a significance that dawns, like the sun, when slow pink overtakes the gray.

People who regularly practice meditation or centering prayer notice differently. The stillness of even a twenty-minute silence sharpens the senses as they return to their duties rested and alert. Awareness shifts. Holy presence is more palpable. Words may acquire more resonance and silence more power. One is slowed into deep receptivity for a time, in a way Wendell Berry describes in his poem "The Peace of Wild Things." When his despair over the world deepens, the speaker seeks the quiet of a place "where the wood drake rests in his beauty on the water, and the great heron feeds." There, he finds, he can "rest in the grace of the world" and be free.

Stillness affords its own kind of freedom. There is great wisdom in the Buddhist admonition "Don't strive. Allow." We may recognize the same teaching in Jesus' invitation to "Consider the lilies of the field" that "toil not, neither do they spin." We are not lilies. But we may, for a time, let them be our teachers.

Friday: Be still before you speak

I have a dear colleague whose notable habit of prolonged silence before speaking has been the subject of both affectionate laughter and admiration. When asked a question, he is likely to stand for what seems a very long moment, maintaining full eye contact, saying nothing. Thinking. His delayed replies are generally thoughtful, sometimes surprising, always gracious. And certainly never hurried.

While such pauses may at times feel a bit socially awkward, they're helpful reminders to slow down and allow a little silence before leaping into speech.

Framed by silence, words may be heard more accurately and attentively. They are likely to be chosen with more care and delivered more comprehensibly. Like the rests in music, silences in conversation allow subtleties of resonance or dimensions of meaning to emerge that might otherwise be missed. They allow for reflection. They allow associations to emerge. Companionable silence is one of the marks of intimacy in friendship—its own reward for a trust that has evolved beyond the need to prove oneself by "protesting too much."

Small silences also offer opportunities to practice the presence of God—to "pray without ceasing." In a heartbeat one can return to center, open again to the Spirit, who dwells within us, receive needed guidance, and let go of whatever is ego-driven or anxious. These things don't happen all the time, or all at once, but the habit of praying in the interstices can lace even the most mundane of tasks with glimmers of divine light.

"I have calmed and quieted my soul," the Psalmist writes. Elsewhere he praises the Lord, who "leads me beside still waters." The theme of quiet that runs through the Psalms underscores its necessity, especially to the poet and singer whose words are rooted in the silence of awestruck contemplation. Without periods of silence, our words become chatter—a chatter encouraged by all our media in our fast-food, fast-word culture where tweets and texts reign. We need places where people gather to encourage one another in silence: centering prayer groups, meditation classes, silent retreats.

Because it is countercultural, the practice of silence can be strenuous. But its rewards are rich, both for the one who waits before speaking and the one who, also waiting, may be surprised by silence into a wholly new kind of hearing.

———

Saturday: Be still until you know

Not all knowledge is incremental. Some things require not only study but trustful periods of expectant waiting. If we are waiting for guidance, a simple prayer—"Show me, guide me, open the ears of my heart"—may punctuate the stillness, but it is in the stillness that knowledge comes. We suddenly know what to do. We know the solution, or the next step. We know what was missing and how to find it.

Intuitive moments, epiphanies, sudden insights don't happen without preparation. An inner stillness is the space into which revelation—new information, an image, a memory, a sense of direction—may come. Those who practice regular meditation or contemplative prayer know that inner stillness isn't blank, but full of awareness, and waiting that isn't passive but an active practice of attentiveness.

The kind of knowing that emerges in that bountiful stillness may not be infallible, but it often comes with startling clarity. And it often comes in the midst of paradox: the most fruitful moments of stillness may be just when haste seems most urgent—when a surgeon is hovering over an organ before cutting, when a sudden traffic decision has to be made, when a small child has clambered onto a dangerous railing and we have to decide how to avoid startling her into falling. The split second between the perception and the act may be a gap wide enough for a beam of guidance. It may be enough to quiet the heart.

"I do hope to die with a quiet heart," John Ames says in Marilynne Robinson's lovely novel *Gilead*. "I know," he adds, "that may not be realistic." Though it seems a modest hope, quieting the heart is not a simple action, but rather a result of focused intention, resistance to distraction, openness to God, willingness to release anxieties and insults, and the long, slow obedience to one of the most insistent commands in Scripture: "Do not be afraid."

A quiet heart is like a clear pool in which one can see the sandy bottom. Fear muddies that clarity. It takes courage to be still long enough for that silt to settle and clarity to come. And it takes patience, which is a form of courage. The quiet heart Ames hopes to die with is a place so secure and so full of knowing that fear can find no place in it.

Follow

   . . . *the rules*

   . . . *before you lead*

. . . *when it's your turn to bring up the rear*

   . . . *your nose*

   . . . *your bliss*

   . . . *leaders you love*

   . . . *the inward path*

Sunday: Follow the rules

I immediately want to modify this suggestion. Follow the rules if they're good. If they apply. Unless they keep you from following a higher law. Until they're no longer life-giving. But remember that grace matters more. Following the rules has gotten a lot of people into deep trouble: people who were just following orders, just doing their job, just not questioning.

Following the rules matters when you're learning to love what the law protects. When you're learning a skill—painting, piano-playing, tennis, creative writing, scientific experimentation—rules keep your lines straight and your colors from running. They get the ball to the other side of the net, the sheet music to sound, and the sentence to make sense. They keep the experiment from blowing up—sometimes literally.

But just beyond the rules lies a play space where rules can be bent and even broken, the moves restyled, the tools put to new purposes, the intuitive leaps honored. If you go there before you've walked the path through the forest of rules, you're likely to be disappointed or hurt or, worse, do damage. If you go there disciplined by the rules, your play will be productive and your efforts richly enjoyable.

In Henry James's novel *The Portrait of a Lady*, an independent-minded young American woman, Isabel, finds that Europeans live by different standards than the people at home. Wanting to find her way in a new culture, she tells her aunt, "I just want to know what the rules are." Her aunt, knowing Isabel's penchant for going her own way, asks, "So that you may follow them?" Isabel's answer has both youth and wisdom in it: "So that I may choose." She knows that without knowing the rules, she's likely to lose her bearings. She also knows that they may not suit her, and in any case that they are not the laws of God, but only of a culture to which she isn't yet certain she wants to belong.

When the laws of God are, in fact, at issue, more is at stake. "You shall follow my rules and keep my statutes and walk in them. I am the Lord your God," we read in Leviticus. God's law is just and righteous, given for guidance in justice and love, gracious enough for David to sing, "Oh, how I love thy law!" So when Jesus breaks the Sabbath, those who love the law are scandalized. They—and we, as we learn to rely more on relationship and less on rules—have to come up against the limits of the law. At the outer edge of those limits stands a person, saying "Follow me. I am the Way."

Once we arrive at that encounter, the journey is less and less about following rules and more and more about the love that is both its motive and its purpose. That journey is also about an attraction so mysterious it can fling away all "thought for the morrow" so that perfectly sane people rise up and, "leaving everything," follow.

Monday: Follow before you lead

Leadership programs and courses and camps and webinars attract thousands of hopeful young people every year. "Everyone is a leader," one brightly colored website declares. And one university assures applicants to their online leadership program that they will "learn to lead on a global scale, and graduate with immediate relevance in the world of global business."

These claims are sweeping indeed. If everyone is a leader, one wonders, who follows? Only those who haven't yet taken the course? If you read the fine print, the real message is somewhat more modest and a little more plausible. Everyone has gifts to be developed. Everyone has creative capacities. Unfortunately, hyperbolic claims about leadership tend to understate the importance of following before you attempt to lead.

I grew up in a generation that was taught early and often to "question authority." It's good advice, but perhaps for a stage of life that comes after one has learned from the authority of parents, teachers, pastors, and mentors. Some of them abuse their authority, to be sure. Recognizing those abuses and naming them is one of the things children need help with from legitimate authority figures. But questioning authority too early can deprive children of the sense of safety that comes with putting oneself in the care of an elder or leader who can provide help along the way.

Any of us could make a list, I imagine, of teachers, leaders, and mentors we've been given along the way and in whose caring company we've learned to come "into our own." The first piano teacher, the scout leader, the "auntie" who invited us into adult conversation. The veteran who took us on as rookies at work; the spiritual directors, formal or informal, who guided us in discernments and decision-making. Most of us have been prepared in periods of following to assume the leadership roles that life has opened up for us.

Preparing young people for leadership involves careful discernment. Have they reached the point where they can lead, or do they need to be held close under the guidance of an elder? Our culture doesn't handle this practice too well; we tend to glorify youth, sometimes to their detriment. We praise originality so early that some miss the dignity and value of taking instruction, imitating, apprenticing, even copying skills that take time to develop. "I'll do it my way" has its place, but first one must have a sense of what it takes to do it at all.

Jesus' call to the disciples, "Follow me," wasn't an invitation to a leadership seminar. For three years he prepared them, sometimes with sharp correction, sometimes letting them wrestle with bewilderment and frustration and fear, for the leadership that came, finally, as a gift from the Holy Spirit in "the fullness of time"—a time that was not theirs to choose, a gift that was, when it came, powerful beyond what they imagined, and wholly entrusted to them because, having been faithful followers, they were ready.

***

Tuesday: Follow when it's your turn to bring up the rear

Somebody has to come behind to make sure no hiker or biker falls by the wayside. Or drive the wagon that picks them up. Or scan for debris and pick up the pieces. The back of the line is an important place of leadership—not glamorous, but necessary. Coming behind the laggers and strays, the reluctant or recalcitrant, requires skills quite different from those required of the biker or hiker in front. The person who brings up the rear doesn't set the pace or make course corrections, and isn't generally surrounded by the most fit, the most competitive, or even the most willing, but by those who may need encouragement or rest or a way to reframe the task.

Yielding control to the one who goes first can be both scary and freeing. Even occupying the rear seat on a tandem bike can be a small exercise in humility that has its reward. The first time my husband and I rented a tandem, the man at the counter warned us, "They call this the 'divorce bike.'" The person in back has to give up control. The person in front starts the turns, makes the quick decisions, and adjusts the gears. But during that first ride, I discovered the paradoxical truth of a line that came to my husband in a dream years ago: "The more I yield, the freer I am." Though one would do well to apply that wisdom selectively, it has its place. There is, as Qoheleth might say, a time to resist and a time to yield. When it's time to yield, yielding can liberate and empower.

To think of the rear, the last in line, as a place of empowerment is its own paradox. But it seems true in many situations that, once one has yielded certain kinds of control or authority or leadership to the one in charge, one is left with a new constellation of possibilities: freed from decision-making, the mind can reflect. Freed from leadership responsibilities, one can enter into conversation with those at the back of the line. The needs of others become apparent from this vantage point in a different way: one can be attentive to who is struggling, who needs to pause, who is getting impatient. And the end of the line is a perfect place to meditate on Jesus' own paradoxical promise that "The last shall be first." In some ways, they already are.

Wednesday: Follow your nose

In the long-ago days before GPS, and before San Francisco became, for me, a navigable city, I got lost among its scary-steep hills without a map. It was evening. I could see the bay and the Transamerica tower, but I didn't know how to get there. (Though a part of the city is a grid, its deceptive diagonals and occasional loops and curves make it hard to plot a course.) I was young and unused to driving in cities, and I had no idea where the nearest gas station might be. I felt a sharp little tug of panic as I paused uneasily on a hilltop and took stock. Then I heard my grandfather's voice: "Just follow your nose."

Grandpa came from the rural South, where imprecise directions seemed mysteriously to get people where they needed to go. "It's just down the road a piece." "It's over yonder." "Not more than a stone's throw away." "Just go round the bend and follow the trace." Traveling through the Carolina outback one year, I was flummoxed more than once by cheerful directions of this kind followed by a wave of the hand as a stranger departed, satisfied he had helped.

But now, in San Francisco, "Follow your nose" suddenly seemed the very best thing to do. "I'm here on a hill," I thought, "and the bay is down there, where I'm looking. Whatever lies between here and there, I'll just go around it or along it until I get there." A deep calm came over me. I wound my slow way through the city on the edge of laughter, so sure, now, that my anxieties were pointless. And I did get to the bay that night, without incident or map.

Years later, a friend came to stay with my family when we were living in a European city. His first morning there, he set out with nothing but a bus schedule and a sack lunch. "Do you want a map?" I asked him. "No, thanks," he cheerfully replied, and explained, "When I get to a new city, the first thing I do is get myself lost. I go somewhere unfamiliar on the bus, get off there, and find my way home. It's a great way to get to know the city." He was back in time for dinner, with topographical information we hadn't acquired in a year of residence.

Maps help, no doubt. But there's something to be said for finding our way by feel, smell, sense of direction, impulse, intuition, or happy accident. What we discover along the way may be exactly what we needed to find.

Thursday: Follow your bliss

We seem to have Joseph Campbell, the Jungian student of mythology and psychology, to thank for this enticing mandate. Like Augustine's "Love and do what you will," it challenges the "shoulds" and "oughts" that so often dominate personal decisions by offering a more internal, subjective, radical understanding of what we need to be faithful to.

"Bliss" may seem a rather lavish, romantic term, but it's a word worth claiming. In Old English it meant, in various contexts, "merriment, happiness, grace, favor." It came from an even older Saxon word that meant "gentle" or "kind." There's great enticement in those words; they invite us to enter into a kind of well-being that's connected to human community and divine love. What gives us that kind of happiness has, as the Quakers might say, "that of God" in it.

Desire—deep, abiding desire, not superficial appetites—is a guide. The occupations and interests that give us energy, the attractions that seem to extend promise and offer empowerment—the longing to paint or dance or dismantle machines and reinvent them or sew or sing or write—any of these may be a path of "bliss," or what in the more traditional Christian language we would call vocation—a calling. Pursuing that bliss may involve a struggle, but only in the paradoxical way Germaine Greer understood when she wrote, "If the struggle isn't joyous, it's the wrong struggle."

"Deep calls to deep," the Psalmist writes. This beautiful

phrase can open various avenues of reflection. I understand it mainly to mean that something deep within us is connected to God, who often speaks to us from the deep places of this world and its wonders—in a corner of a sunlit forest, in the radiance of a painting, in the elegant ways math makes sense of things, in a haunting line of music.

What summons us out of longing into delight is something to pay attention to, with discernment and trust that God wills our happiness and that following the way we are given, whatever struggle it entails, will be the path of bliss.

Friday: Follow leaders you love

I used to say of my favorite professor, "I'd have taken any course he taught—even advanced calculus." Coming from me, that was high praise indeed. Advanced calculus wasn't my idea of a good time—or a good grade. But his teaching seemed to me always to incite and invite more imagination and discovery than I or my classmates realized we were capable of.

The best teaching and learning take place in a climate of love—love of learning itself, and a particular kind of love between the one who teaches and the one who is taught, rooted in respect and gratitude on both sides, and perhaps a little awe at the epiphanies one can prepare for but not force. Teachers lead, students follow, yet the relationship at its best is a deep collaboration and partnership in learning.

We find the teachers we need along the way, not always in the classroom. During each season of life, if we're open to finding them, people emerge who can help us along the path. This seems to me as true for us collectively as individually. In local government, on school boards, in NGOs, in churches, leaders emerge whom we recognize as fit and timely blessings for the community. Ideally, their authority is publicly acknowledged; often, though, leaders with real spiritual authority work from the margins or under the radar. To follow them means departing from the way of the crowd. Dropping our nets, as the disciples did, and going.

The nuns who followed Mother Teresa, the marchers who followed Martin Luther King, the young people who follow Jean Vanier and live in l'Arche communities, the peacemaking teams who come alongside those living in combat zones, and millions of others who have joined ranks in response to imaginative, open-hearted leaders have found their own way through their following of others. In our culture, following gets bad press; young people are urged from all sides to become leaders when, in fact, they might be better advised for a time to look for the leaders they can trust, love, and learn from.

The amazing empowerment of the disciples in the book of Acts didn't happen by magic, but by the slow miracle that unfolded over hours and days of following, listening, accepting correction, enduring painful bewilderment, and loving, often in spite of themselves. They had found the leader they loved, recognized him, and were compelled by the one who called himself "the Way." "To whom else shall we go?" Peter replied, when Jesus asked the Twelve, "Do you want to go away as well?" Jesus was the leader Peter loved, and the leader whose divine identity he recognized. Leaders who follow him are worth following.

～

Saturday: Follow the inward path

"Don't just go on," I tell my students in literature courses. "Go in." Pause where the story or poem gives you pause, and reflect on what stopped you and why—what the writer did, what it evoked. Poems and stories invite us to notice our felt responses, to reflect on where moments in our lives resemble those of the speaker, to experience the flicker of memory and association when we encounter particular words and images, to pay attention to what is triggered, to experiment with empathy. The good ones stop us, or at least tug at us to slow us down. They invite us inward.

All the arts do this in their own ways. Vermeer's *Girl with a Pearl Earring*, Rembrandt's many self-portraits, Van Gogh's *Starry Night*, and even Jackson Pollock's sweeping entanglements invite us to do the inner work of allowing ourselves to be addressed, challenged, and changed. A friend of mine played a game with her children they called "pop in." When they looked at a painting, they would "pop in" to the place depicted and talk about what might be just around the corner or over the hill or in the next room.

In a course called "Contemplative Reading," I asked students to listen to short musical pieces and pay attention to the "interior space" they opened up. Where did the music take them? I asked. How might they describe the architecture or landscape of that interior space? To do this exercise, they needed to appropriate certain kinds of music as tools for guided meditation. It yielded surprising and gratifying moments of intimate sharing: we were led into conversations that were no longer simply "academic," but those of pilgrims on an inward path.

A therapist I worked with years ago frequently nudged me to "Go to the place in you that knows." Though we didn't share a common spiritual tradition, his advice helped me return to my own sacred inner space—the "room" where I meet God in prayer, where I receive guidance, where I am restored by deep quiet, where I may be visited by divine Presence.

We often need the help of that prompt—someone who will simply smile and point us back onto the inward path when we're wandering down rabbit trails. When we re-emerge from the journey inward, having dwelt a while in the place where that path leads, we may find ourselves richly prepared for the journey ahead.

Rejoice

... *greatly*

... *in the Lord*

... *in unlikely circumstances*

"... *though you have considered all the facts*"

... *in others' happiness*

... *against the odds*

... *while the light lasts*

Sunday: Rejoice greatly

On his recent visit to the United States, Pope Francis began a homily by reminding Christians to rejoice:

> Paul tells us to rejoice; he practically orders us to rejoice. This command resonates with the desire we all have for a fulfilling life, a meaningful life, a joyful life. . . . Something deep within us invites us to rejoice and tells us not to settle for placebos, which simply keep us comfortable.

I love the idea that we've been "ordered" to rejoice— that joy is commanded and expected of people of faith because it is the logical, natural outcome of faith. And that joy has little to do with satisfied appetites or creature comforts.

The liturgical year marks out festival days on which joy is expressed and expected. Transcending individual sorrows and sharing in communal rejoicing are ways of proclaiming something fundamentally true: that we have reason to rejoice. That joy has the last word. That it is bigger than sorrow.

Rejoicing is also bigger than excitement. "Excited" is an overused word in some circles: we have "exciting" programs or prospects for upcoming events, we're "excited" about what the youth are doing on their mission trip, and we're all expected to be "excited" to hear this week's speaker or young musician. It's easy to mistake excitement or enthusiasm for joy.

It helps to remember that joy, even great joy, is sometimes quiet. Because joy isn't just an emotion—it's a way of knowing. "All joy reminds," C. S. Lewis wrote in *Surprised by Joy*. It confirms what we know and believe most deeply about who God is and who we are created to be. And it reminds us that we were loved into being, that we are accompanied and watched over on our journeys, that all our sufferings in this life will melt into unimaginable delight when we "arrive where we started."

Great rejoicing is, in the decorous words of the old Book of Common Prayer, a "meet and right" response to God's love and the gift of life. In his farewell discourse in John 15 to the disciples, Jesus' tenderness becomes as explicit as anywhere in the Gospels. He assures them that as they follow his way, they will abide in his love just as he abides in God's love. He completes his assurances with these words: "These things I have spoken to you, that my joy may be in you, and that your joy may be full." Joy is the objective, the hope, the evidence, and the outcome of a life lived in God's love, burning brilliant as gold in fire even in the very midst of sorrow.

Monday: Rejoice in the Lord

When he was about four and attending a Baptist preschool, our grandson left a phone message for us that we saved for many months and listened to when we needed a cheering moment. In his piping little voice, with great conviction and without even a prefatory "Hello," he recited, "'Rejoice in the Lord *always*. Again I say, rejoice.' Philippians 4:4." That was it. The whole message. Quite sufficient, especially with the particular emphasis on "always" that made the familiar line into a sermon.

"Always" is a tall order—really a little more than most of us can manage. If one were really to rejoice "always," one would have to live at a different altitude—one that offered a much wider perspective on the hairpin turns and frequent setbacks of adult life. Rejoicing in the midst of depression (economic or psychological), or failure or disappointment, or when the world just seems like a strange and dangerous place—rejoicing at these times has to mean something more complicated than feeling happy.

There are many moments, as we all know, when the well-meant advice to "count your blessings" just seems like a pious cliché, more irritating than helpful. Rejoicing at those times may mean something more like simply remembering—reaching for the deep knowing that lies buried just below consciousness, down in the precincts of primal memory, that we are made by Love and return to Love, that God is our light and our salvation, that even when we can't see how it's true, we can accept St. Julian's assurance that "All shall be well, and all manner of thing shall be well."

Some days, rejoicing may be no more than a recitation of those comforts we cling to even though they seem cold. "What is our only comfort in life and death?" the Heidelberg catechism asks, and the answer follows: "That I am not my own, but belong with body and soul, both

in life and in death, to my faithful Savior Jesus Christ."
This answer goes well beyond "There, there." Instead of a
cheering word, we are given a theological claim—a fact. As
a British friend of mine might say, "There you are, then."

If the truth sets us free, it also enables us to rejoice, because joy is a form of knowing. To be joyful is to rest in a
kind of certainty that doesn't depend on human standards
of evidence, but upon an understanding that is a gift of
the Holy Spirit, freely given to those willing to receive
it. If we open our hearts to it, not only peace that passes
understanding, but joy that passes rational explanation
can come flooding in, even in the worst of times.

***

Tuesday: Rejoice in unlikely circumstances

"But to rejoice when no one else is there/is even harder
than it is to weep," W. H. Auden writes in a poem I have
long loved. Celebration is generally a seasonal matter and
takes place in community, but sometimes our joys come
in ways that can't be shared for reasons of discretion,
or at times when others' sorrow makes it appropriate to
postpone festivity, or when it might seem we ought to be
wrapped in a mantle of sobriety for a solemn occasion.

Still, it is possible to rejoice in the very midst of weeping at a friend's funeral, or when a rejection letter arrives,
or when an unexpected divorce reframes one's whole
sense of the future. I've known people who have had those
very counterintuitive experiences. Joy came upon them,

unexpected as a shaft of sunlight in a frigid landscape, as they got a glimpse of something for which loss made way, something being prepared for them even in the midst of loss. What was taken made room for what was given; those who mourned were blessed.

We can't, of course, manufacture joy for ourselves in such unlikely and unwelcome circumstances. All we can do is allow for it. The allowing is a spiritual discipline, and doesn't become habitual without a sustained practice of opening the heart and the imagination to divine possibilities. One way to cultivate this practice is to step back from whatever is happening and ask, as a Quaker friend of mine frequently does, "I wonder what this is about?" Simple as it seems, the question reshapes anxiety into a lively curiosity. It can neutralize threat and disappointment and turn them to detached, confident expectation. It can soften an outcry into a simple question.

The assumption behind the question is that all we undergo or witness is "about" something larger. Life is rich with meaning, and all stories may be read as parables, all stoppages as lyrical moments. What is dry or depressing or boring or seemingly unbearable may be relieved, if not wholly removed, by the slight shift of perspective a question can offer, like a window which, when opened, lets in light from a new angle that changes the ways in which we see.

Wednesday: Rejoice, "though you have considered all the facts"

Let's face it, friends: the facts are grim. The list of facts we need to consider to live responsibly on the planet at this point in its complicated history is long. Global temperatures are rising; weather phenomena are becoming more extreme; species are becoming extinct at an unprecedented rate; rainforests are disappearing; slavery has not been abolished; extreme poverty continues; innocent people are killed and their homes destroyed when the wealthy go to wars in which truth, it seems, is still the "first casualty." Some days it's hard to read the news without feeling overwhelmed.

Wendell Berry, whose poem "Manifesto, Mad Farmer: Liberation Front" includes the line I use as the title of this piece, is one who does consider all those facts. He has spoken prophetically to more than one generation of Americans about environmental and economic disasters wrought by greed, short-sightedness, and the substitution of "ownership" for "stewardship" as a goal for personal and corporate life. He speaks about soil depletion, mountaintop removal, the consequences of losing relationship to the earth and natural processes, overconsumption, and community.

Berry also writes luminous poetry that invites readers to delight in the deep pleasures of long marriage and friendship, in Sabbath rest, in "the peace of wild things," in language and song and story. His life work offers a rich example of what it means to rejoice "though you have considered all the facts."

That is not a line to be read glibly; it was not written glibly. Joy that survives all the bleak statistics doesn't come cheap. It is the fruit of practical faith—the kind of faith Berry attested to when he observed that "Work done faithfully and well is prayer." Joy is also the fruit of endurance and patience, fostered in communities of people who care for each other, laughing over each other's foibles, listening to each other's stories, investing in each other's children, grieving each other's losses, living together "through tragedy into celebration and joy."

This kind of rejoicing may be possible only in the context of human connections forged and tended in love. It may be possible only by clinging to Jesus' mysterious promise and assurance: "In the world you will have tribulation. But take heart; I have overcome the world." In light of that, we can afford to consider all the facts.

Thursday: Rejoice in others' happiness

Among the people I most deeply admire are those who take genuine delight in other people's accomplishments or good fortune, even when they themselves are not being similarly blessed. I think of colleagues who are the first to congratulate the one awarded "Professor of the Year," of a young woman who still longed for a successful pregnancy beaming at a friend's new baby, of a remarkable young man actually pleased to be beaten at his own favorite sport by "someone so good."

Occasionally I have that experience. Sometimes, when I'm reading another writer's work, instead of thinking wistfully, "I wish I'd written that," I feel the deep pleasure of her sentences lift my spirits beyond the reach of envy. I want that response to others' pleasures as well, when they receive, achieve, or create something I can't. It's much more satisfying than envy or comparison of any kind.

The attitude I'm describing isn't the result of a decision to be generous-minded so much as the result of a deep, consistently fostered, prayerful understanding that to love my neighbor as myself is to reckon my own happiness as inseparable from his or hers. In a sense, it is to love my neighbor because she *is* my self: our fortunes, our social web, our DNA, the very stardust of which we're made links us together in ways that transcend conscious reckoning and literalize what can sound like a romantic abstraction: that we are one.

When I am happy for others' happiness, I get to participate in that happiness in a way that's impossible when I'm clenched with envy, jealousy, or competitiveness. "There is no competition in the kingdom of heaven," one poet has written—a truth and a hope that ought to make us wonder, at least, about what rampant capitalism has normalized. In the so-called free market, "competitive" is a term of approbation and a status devoutly to be wished. Children are taught from the time they hit their first T-ball to compete, admonitions to good sportsmanship notwithstanding. Investment in winning, in beating the opposite team, grows to such a frenzy among professional sports fans that it sometimes leads to violence at public games. This isn't a climate in which rejoicing over others' successes gets ready support or approval.

All the more reason, then, for people who profess faith in an exuberantly, luminously countercultural Jewish laborer to cultivate practices and attitudes of collaboration over competition, and appreciation over envy. Like the exercises that strengthen competitive athletes' muscles, small acts of appreciation, multiplied, make for strong, capacious hearts and enable a depth and range of happiness one's own successes simply can't provide.

Friday: Rejoice against the odds

I've always found the expression "hope against hope" a little puzzling. We use it to mean hoping against all odds, hoping in desperate situations. It calls us, as Scripture so often does, into paradox: over against the hope that seems already to have been defeated, find a new kind of hope, a way to hope on new terms, a way that reframes the very idea of hope.

The same might be said about rejoicing. Stories about the lives of people of great faith almost invariably include situations in which joy emerges in the very midst of deep sorrow—a kind of joy that defies common sense and emotional logic, and that may almost seem a little offensive to conventional pieties. I think, for instance, of Horatio Spafford, who wrote the hymn "It Is Well with My Soul" after personal tragedy struck twice. He lost most of his worldly wealth, invested in real estate, in the great Chicago fire in 1871. Then, detained by business, he sent his wife and four daughters ahead of him to Europe, but lost all of his daughters when the ship sank; only his wife survived.

That Spafford could write a hymn in those circumstances, a hymn whose rolling refrain is a repetition of the confident line "It is well, it is well with my soul," seems truly remarkable—and counterintuitive. He was moved to write it, the story goes, as his own ship passed the site where the earlier vessel had gone down. Such an impulse hardly seems possible apart from the Holy Spirit, in whom all things are possible.

But this is, in fact, what we're called to: radical trust, radical hope, radical rejoicing, in spite of all that by human standards makes any of those attitudes seem unlikely, and even impertinent. Rejoicing in ways that make no common sense—only uncommon sense. "Joy" is one of those overused words, like "love," that has become something of a Christian cliché. It needs to be retrieved from trivial use and put on a higher shelf, because the call to rejoice is a high and challenging calling—one we live into as faith deepens and matures, one that takes us beyond measurable happiness. We can't manufacture that kind of joy—we can only prepare to be surprised by it.

Saturday: Rejoice while the light lasts

Many of us know Dylan Thomas's youthful admonition to his dying father not to "go gentle into that good night," but to "Rage, rage against the dying of the light." It appealed to me in my own youth as a heroic attitude that claimed and affirmed life over against the curse of death until its very end. I still admire the energy of that will to live out the life we're given. I admire the determination of those I've known who have found ways to wring the last juice out of life despite physical diminishment and debility. Still, the "rage" has lost some of its appeal.

What the "rage" rightly recalls is that death is the primal curse. As a pastor friend of ours put it when he preached his mother's funeral sermon, "Death stinks." The reassuring pieties we may utter at the time of death about going to a better place have their place, but that death is a strenuous passage, a costly condition of human life, a source of keen suffering, and a curse whose "sting" lingers even for those who believe it has been overcome once for all. So death should not be leapt over too quickly. Its emotional reality is complex in the best of cases.

But that complexity, for people of faith, includes a place to rejoice, even on the final stretch of the journey. In my work as a hospice volunteer, I have been humbled and edified to witness the courage of people who know their last day is near, and even though the dear natural light of the world they love will soon be extinguished, they find reasons to rejoice. Small things make them glad—visits, flowers, a New Yorker cartoon, a favorite psalm, a funny story from the outside world, a grandchild's success, a word game, a hug. There is a generosity in their willingness to receive pleasure and even joy at that very outer edge of the life they've known.

From them I've learned what it can mean to believe and claim the truth that every day is a gift, and that grace is possible and available even in the final hours. At such a time one may rejoice mainly in imminent release from pain, but faith offers reasons beyond that. As some have testified who have been to that edge and back, new dimensions of awareness and hope may emerge only then, when (to quote Hopkins), "though the last lights off the black West went/Oh, morning, at the brown brink eastward, springs." In such a moment it takes only a turning to see that we go from light to light.

Ask

. . . for what you need

. . . for what you want

. . . for what you cannot predict

. . . knowing yes can be harder than no

. . . without an agenda

. . . on others' behalf

. . . for what is altered in fulfillment

Sunday: Ask for what you need

Ask and you shall receive. It sounds like a fairly simple directive, but we all know the ways it doesn't work. It's not a magic formula. One way to understand that bold invitation to "Ask and it shall be given to you" is to look at the context in which Jesus issued it to his disciples. They had been with him for a long period of basic training in a new spirituality, the like of which they'd never experienced before. Their habits, their assumptions, their theology, and even their desires were being transformed. And that's the thing: when one's desires are no longer driven by superficial, culture-bound, itchy wants-of-the-moment, when they've become deeply aligned with the divine Spirit, who moves us gently and persistently toward the persons we were created to be, our sense of what we "need" will be defined by the desires that are rooted in our deepest purposes.

"O, reason not the need!" King Lear cries when his cruel daughter insists he doesn't need his retinue of servants. "Allow not nature more than nature needs,/man's life is cheap as beast's." In other words—and Lear makes a good point—to grow our humanity, rejoice in life, be fully ourselves, we need something more than bare necessity. We need the extra wine at the wedding in Cana. We need the twelve extra baskets of bread. When I was growing up, attending one English class after another, I found Lear's line a fair complement and challenge to Thoreau's equally compelling insistence on the dangers of superfluity.

The simplicity of Jesus (the Son of Man, who had "no-where to lay his head") and the abundance of God (the One whom poet Robinson Jeffers described as being inclined to "fling rainbows over the rain") remind us to hold in lively creative tension the needs and desires that make us human. They remind us to recognize that even in deprivation, without being glib about the horrors humans may endure, we have access to what we need, if we ask, and that God's will for us does and will finally far exceed what we can imagine asking.

—

Monday: Ask for what you want

This, I learned, is the secret of healthy assertiveness. On a road trip my daughter and I listened to a series of "assertiveness training" classes which taught us that healthy assertiveness doesn't mean learning to say "No" so much as learning to identify what you want and ask for it, and being willing to accept "No" for an answer. When you ask for what you want, the teacher pointed out, you often get it, and even when you don't, you let those who love you know you a little better.

What you want has a lot to do with who you are. If you ask a child what she wants for her birthday, her list will tell you a lot about her—her developmental stage, her susceptibility to peer pressure, her growing edge, her curiosities, even what she may be avoiding and where she may need encouragement.

Asking can be a healthy way of exploring your own desires. Sometimes hearing yourself ask helps clarify how much you really want what you're asking for, or even whether you really do. An old want may have faded; a thoughtful response may modify the wanting. Asking may also give you training in much-needed candor: relationships founder because people don't feel free either to say what they want or to say no. If both people can do both those things honestly, courteously, and trustingly, the relationship can grow strong and resilient.

Learning to take "No" for an answer may be the most strenuous part of the training, but it's a significant part. If we're not crushed or embarrassed or angered or silenced by a simple "No," we may find that refusals provide important guidance. The adage that "When God closes a door, he opens a window" has its very human counterpart. If one avenue of possibility is refused, we get a chance to imagine and experiment with alternatives.

My favorite among the assertiveness exercises was simply to make a "want list" to share with a partner or friend. All the wants. The whole wish list. The trips, the appliances, the event tickets, the services, the personal assistant, the cool motorbike, the high-end hiking boots, the open-ended time and the quiet and the company you want but haven't asked for. You won't get all of it. But you might get some of it.

Barbara Ras's delightful poem "You Can't Have It All" begins and ends with that refrain, but in between is a long, lovely list of what you can have:

But you can have the fig tree and its fat leaves like
    clown hands
gloved with green. You can have the touch of a single
    eleven-year-old finger
on your cheek, waking you at one a.m. to say the
    hamster is back.
You can have the purr of the cat and the soulful look
of the black dog, the look that says, If I could I would
    bite
every sorrow until it fled, and when it is August,
you can have it August and abundantly so. . . .

And so the poem continues, reminding us that we can't
have it all, but also reminding us how much we *can* have,
and concluding wisely that you can't have it all, "but there
is this." The poem tells us—and faith tells us—that the
"this" we can have is various and abundant indeed.

—

Tuesday: Ask for what you cannot predict

Fear of the unknown looms large. Few of us sail into the
future without some attempt to assess the risks and gauge
the probabilities. And I imagine that few of us relish those
moments when we have to make a decision despite in-
complete information.

    Paul's challenging instruction to "give thanks in all cir-
cumstances" and his encouragement to "be content" in all
situations can be helpful exactly then, when circumstance

finds us at the edge of a dark wood. To live at that level of radical trust requires an open heart and a practice of praying without ceasing—living in daily communion with the Spirit, who guides us through the roughest waters.

To pray, as many of us do every week, "Thy will be done" is to ask for what we cannot predict. The prayer focuses our asking on the desire for alignment with divine will, not a particular goal or object. I don't believe this prayer forecloses the practice of praying very specifically for what we want, but it does push us beyond the limits of our own imagination and desires toward openness to God's surprises. That God works by surprise is abundantly evident in Jesus' complex ministry, which was so often witty, subversive, inventive, paradoxical, and sudden.

The willingness to be surprised requires the willingness to give up control. I admire a friend's ready response to queries about what she wants for her birthday: "Surprise me!" It's not because she's unwilling to name what she wants, but because she enjoys entrusting her pleasure to others' imaginations. Offering someone else a choice in matters that affect us is a generous practice of love and trust that can deepen pleasure on both sides of a relationship.

But even in intimate relationship it takes a bit of courage to do this. Surprises can go awry. Good intentions can go wrong. And letting go leads to unpredictable outcomes. "Thy will be done" is a leap of faith—every time. But that leap keeps us fit to run the course.

Wednesday: Ask, knowing yes can be harder than no

Popular sayings got that way because there's some wisdom in them. One of those is the paradoxical warning "Be careful what you ask for; you might get it." And sometimes we ask for the challenges we get.

An extreme example that comes to mind is a hospice patient I visited—a devout Catholic woman with a virulent and painful form of cancer who told me she had prayed that the Lord would "give me my purgatory here." Hers is not a spirituality or an understanding of the afterlife I subscribe to, but I still admired her gutsy request. It came, I learned, from a desire to go directly to God. Hers was a love that fully embraced the suffering she believed came with it. I can only hope my love of God might be as simple and whole-hearted as hers.

I think also of people who have adopted children with special needs, knowing even as they hoped and prayed for the children who needed them that their lives would be circumscribed by those needs and their limits regularly tested. They asked out of a clear sense of vocation and prayerful discernment that preceded the bold request for what most couples might pray to be spared.

Love faces and even invites challenges, not in a spirit of arrogant presumption ("I can handle this") but out of a desire to grow larger, more pliant to divine will, more capacious in trust. Sometimes it is pure love that asks, "May I carry this burden for you?" "May I stay with you while you die?" "May I visit you every week in prison?" "May I come with the disaster relief team?" "May I volunteer in the detention center?" "May I stay with the Alzheimer's patient while her spouse takes a weekend off?" "May I help you?"

That last is such a simple question, often asked as a courteous gesture. But if we mean it, it's a door to adventures in consent, and perhaps to a generosity that grows when it is stretched.

———

Thursday: Ask without an agenda

I have one acquaintance whose questions feel like interrogations. Somehow they make me defensive because I sense that they come from an anxious desire to control. I have another acquaintance whose questions make me feel deeply attended to, listened to. I feel as though she awaits my answers with open-hearted interest—that her questions come from a desire to know me better. Recognizing my responses to these two kinds of questions has taught me to consider where my own questions are coming from. Why do I ask? Is it for the sake of deepening relationship, or for the sake of keeping tabs and controlling?

The reasons we ask questions vary widely. We ask because we want information. Or because we want to keep conversation going with someone whose company we enjoy. We ask because we wonder how our point of view compares with someone else's. Or because we're open to being persuaded. Or as a set-up for our own efforts to persuade. We ask because we want to express interest, or to be an object of someone's interest. We ask because a question is a teaching device. Or because a question opens a door to learning.

An honest question is one without a specific agenda— open-ended, open-hearted, curious, designed to invite an honest answer, and to give that answer the time it takes. It's hard to ask honest questions when we're in a hurry. "How are you?" has become, on many fleeting occasions, a gesture like a quick wave that's not intended to bring forth real information. It's also so general as to be dis-abling. When I'm asked, I have to quickly decide whether to give a health update, a mood update, a report on the day's progress, or the common one-word response (which I choose most often): "Fine. How are you?"

If I sense that someone's asking me a question with an agenda behind it—especially if I think they're being nosy or controlling, or gathering material for gossip—I have to discern whether I owe them the information. It took me a long time to recognize that being "open and honest" didn't necessarily mean delivering any and all information someone asked for. Discretion is a valuable protection for what may need protecting. We're not required to submit indiscriminately to others' judgments.

Nor are we in a position to make judgments. Asking without an agenda means putting aside our tendencies to judge and going "unarmed" into the conversation, willing to hear, willing to consider, willing to ask more, willing to bring our imaginations to bear on others' points of view.

It means remembering that we never know the whole story, that we must be ready to offer interest and acceptance and, where we differ, to offer our point of view without making it our business to expose or humiliate or defeat. Debate has its place, and good, disciplined debate has tremendous social value, but most conversations serve others and God more richly when they don't degenerate into contests.

Friday: Ask on others' behalf

I've written more letters of recommendation than I care to count for students applying to graduate schools, jobs, internships. Occasionally I make a phone call on their behalf, asking someone to recognize a special circumstance or give particular consideration to someone whose transcript might not reflect their unusual gifts.

Others have done the same for me. When, in my last year of grad school, a kindly professor offered to call a friend on the faculty of a school where I was applying for a job, I demurred, thinking that wasn't quite fair. He sat me down and said, "I'm not asking him to bypass proper procedure—just to notice you. All professional transactions take place between human beings who want to give each other a little help where they can. It's a service to him to help him in the sorting process by pointing out someone he might not want to miss." I took that to heart. In healthy communities we speak, write, ask, and pray on others' behalf all the time.

Intercessory prayer is one of the most important ways that faith communities sustain their common life. Asking for healing or blessing or forgiveness on others' behalf is a direct response to the commandment to love our neighbors as ourselves. As members of the same body, they are, in a broad and mysterious sense, ourselves. We are members of one another. Knowing that makes it clear that taking another person's concerns to heart—taking them personally—means sharing responsibility for their welfare, casting our lot with them, getting in the same boat.

Somewhere along the line I picked up this simple bit of common wisdom: "Everybody does better when everybody does better." The rich don't really benefit when the poor are oppressed. The community isn't healthier when the renegade is punished and cast out rather than reconciled, though reconciliation may be more arduous, confusing, and painful in the short run. When we pray for our enemies, there's something in it for us. Asking forgiveness and renewal on their behalf may open our hearts and imaginations a little wider, and enable us to find a deeper humility.

Asking on another's behalf may even mean asking in their stead. One of the wonderful mysteries of faith is that another has been judged in our place. And we, mysteriously, can do something of that kind for each other. In Acts, an angel promises Cornelius that Peter will come to him with "a message by which you will be saved, you and all your household." That final phrase "and all your household" occurs numerous times in Scripture, serving to remind us that we're on this journey together, bound by blood, tribe, calling, common needs, common ills, common resources. And, at our best, we are bound in a chorus of prayer in which the words we speak on our own behalf mingle almost indistinguishably with those we speak for others.

———

Saturday: Ask for what is altered in fulfillment

Among my favorite lines from T. S. Eliot's rich, challenging, mystical poem "Little Gidding" are these:

And what you thought you came for
Is only a shell, a husk of meaning
From which the purpose breaks only when it is
    fulfilled
If at all. Either you had no purpose
Or the purpose is beyond the end you figured
And is altered in fulfillment. . . .

We don't know what we're being prepared for. At any given time, we have only a partial understanding of what we're about, what our work will enable or promote, how we're participating in designs greater and grander than our own goals. We enter into conversations, projects, conferences, contracts, and relationships with our own intentions and hopes, but if we're adults, we've lived long enough to know how those change along the way.

What we thought marriage would be like is never quite

what we experience. What we thought we would be contributing to the company changes as the market shifts. What we thought our education was preparing us for turns out to be something quite different. Robert Frost writes about how one may stand before "two roads diverg[ing] in a yellow wood," knowing "how way leads on to way." The road that "goes ever on and on" (as Tolkien describes it) is rarely a straight line.

So when we ask for our hopes to be fulfilled or our intentions to come to fruition, it might be wise to keep in mind that those intentions themselves will likely be "altered in fulfillment." We may find that something quite different from what we thought we wanted was, in fact, what we needed after all. Parents of children with disabilities, partners of spouses with painful pasts, pastors of congregations with hidden wounds—all of them learn this. What they have they wouldn't have known to ask for, wouldn't perhaps have had the courage to ask for, but when it is given, it becomes a vocation to live into with unexpected blessings, though they may come with unwanted challenges.

Our purposes are always "beyond the end we figured." This is good news. What is unfolding, lotus-like, around us is a kaleidoscopic design to which every generation and every life add rich new colors. To ask for what is altered in fulfillment is to acquiesce joyfully to a human condition of uncertainty that is a prerequisite for divine surprise.

Dare

. . . to face the future

. . . to consider others' judgments

. . . to admit honest failure

. . . to confront your inner critic

. . . to protest abuse of power

. . . to speak when it's called for

. . . to endure what you must

Sunday: Dare to face the future

Obviously, this is easier said than done. There's plenty to be afraid of in the future that scientists and economists predict. Here's a short list: nuclear holocaust; drought and water wars; decimation of species; economic meltdown; progressive militarization; violence in schools; pesticides; guns in the wrong hands. And so on. Most of us have our lists, and they sometimes motivate us to act—to sign petitions, contribute money, watch documentaries, write corporate leaders and Congress people, pray. They may also keep us in a chronic state of more or less suppressed anxiety.

So we look for reasons to hope—even to rejoice. Wendell Berry's advice, quoted earlier—Rejoice, "though you have considered all the facts"—is exactly what faith challenges us to do: to look largely enough at the human story to understand that we are involved in an unfolding of events that transcends human history even as it dignifies the human journey with a meaning that goes beyond what we imagine and finally absorbs and abolishes all the human suffering that darkens this Valley of the Shadow. There is comfort in Tolkien's conviction that the earthly narrative is ultimately a "eucatastrophe"—the happy opposite of catastrophe, whose outcome is figured forth in the heavenly banquet, the wolf lying down with the lamb, laughter, story, and song.

These are not sentimental fictions, but articles of faith. Yet even though we believe them, fear of the future doesn't generally melt away under their heavenly rays. We

179

still live with day-to-day dangers, fears for our children, apprehensions about money, chemicals, contaminants, racism, violence, and ignorance. So we need practical strategies for dispelling the garden-variety anxieties that drain energy and erode joy and keep us from daring to do what we're called to do.

One of those strategies is to practice presence. That is, to practice the presence of God, and to practice dwelling deeply and intentionally in the present moment. The eternal moment is now. To be fully present is to live fully in humanity and radical trust.

When Jesus advises his followers to "take no thought for the morrow" and invites them to "consider the lilies of the field" that neither toil nor spin, he is encouraging them to dwell in that state of trust. Not necessarily to make no plans or forgo preparation for foreseeable difficulties, but to rest in God's own assurance of provision, guidance, and the grace to endure. He does not promise a rose garden; he does promise a resurrection.

While we remain on this journey—for some a much harder one than for others—we have these assurances, which came to me vividly in prayer one time when I sorely needed them: *You are held. You are witnessed. You are accompanied. You are loved.* We still do well to carry first-aid kits and use water purifiers and lock our doors and work our hardest to end the poverty that is a taproot of violence. But, ultimately, we don't need to be afraid. We can dare to lift our gaze and scan the dark horizon. Death and disaster will never be the final word.

Monday: Dare to consider others' judgments

"I don't care what other people think" is easy to say, but harder to feel, because it's seldom true. In my experience it's a claim often made in an effort to *make* it true.

Many of us carry memories of parents' or teachers' or friends' judgments—old wounds that still make us hypersensitive to criticism. We may have learned to receive it without protest, but still find that it stings. If the old wounds haven't healed, we may feel we can't afford to open ourselves to anything that might reawaken this pain.

In the early years of my professional life, a mentor of mine taught me the wisdom that lies in the word "afford." "You can afford to let that go," she would say. Or "You can afford to give it some time." Or "You can afford to try that out and see what happens." The word was a reminder of a truth that moved me beyond fear and defensiveness on many occasions—that I had access to spiritual resources so rich and reliable, I didn't have to grasp or clutch or hoard or defend. I could afford to be generous in my judgments, open-hearted in my listening, quick in my apologies and my forgiveness. I was rich in love, and secure.

I can afford to consider others' judgments when I hold my own with comfortable conviction—willing to change if evidence provides a reason to do so, but also having considered my position or course of action carefully enough not to feel it will crumble at the first sign of conflict. Self-examination and an appetite for learning both help keep me receptive to what might be learned even in ways or from people I find difficult.

The wisdom I've been taught doesn't mean I don't recoil or react badly on occasion, but it does give me the solid ground of good spiritual counsel, and a plumb line when things go emotionally askew. I'm reminded that because I don't need to be afraid of what others think, I can entertain criticism in a spirit of openness to learning, recognizing that sometimes our critics are our teachers. I can afford to hear them, step back, and consider the merit of their judgments. I may even end up thanking them.

Tuesday: Dare to admit honest failure

On one Sunday a month for a year, volunteers in our church were invited to share personal stories about gifts in their lives. One of the most memorable was a story about failure. With both humility and humor, a lively, lovely woman most of us would have described as a remarkable success in personal relationships and professional accomplishment talked about a year in her life when failure overtook her on several fronts at once. Her husband left; confusions and complications at work put a dent in her career; her attempts to lose weight foundered in the midst of stress; investments tanked. Her story was one of amazing grace—not a simplistic or even simple account of miraculous recoveries, but a story about faith tested and deepened, about help from unexpected sources, about friends' fidelity, about discovering resilience she didn't know she had.

Her story also reframed failure. It can sound (and be) glib to call crisis an opportunity or a gift, or to insist on silver linings or hidden blessings when disaster hits and hopes are dashed and honest efforts yield nothing. People who rush in too quickly with those reassurances, however true they might ultimately be, are often, understandably, unwelcome. Our storyteller acknowledged that. She didn't avoid the pain, the losses, the days when comfort seemed cold and prayer dry and possibilities remote. But she did conclude that failure is a teacher and can be a gift.

It taught her that she could survive. It gave her a chance to develop resilience and resourcefulness, to rely on old friends and develop new ones, to renew her faith on more complex terms, to recognize her privilege, to enter into mourning and find its blessings.

It seems that most published biographies tell stories of failure. Some of the more famous are those of Lincoln (he suffered eight political defeats before being elected president), Beethoven (his music teacher thought he was hopeless at composition), Babe Ruth (he struck out 1,330 times), and Michael Jordan (he missed more than 9,000 shots, lost almost 300 games). It's heartening to read these, and also to read the Gospels and remember how even the disciples closest to Jesus failed him and themselves at the most crucial moments in history, but rose out of that by grace to live lives of power and wisdom and great faith.

I'm not sure I believe the greeting-card assurance that

"If you're not afraid to fail, there's nothing you can't accomplish." But I do believe that if you're not afraid to fail, you'll multiply opportunities not only to succeed, but to receive the amazing grace we live by.

~

Wednesday: Dare to confront your inner critic

My inner critic is alive and well. He (for some reason that carping voice in my head is masculine) still shows up in the midst of preparations for public speaking, or mid-paragraph on a morning when I've started to feel happy about the march of sentences across the page. Or he comes after the performance, or even after publication, bringing his wet blanket and withering eye to point out where I mumbled or misspoke. *Your sentences are too long. You spoke too fast. The woman in the back corner left early, and someone in the third row nodded off. Annie Dillard said it more elegantly. Anne Lamott is wittier. And who are you to write about spirituality on a day awash with drivel and distractions?* My inner critic has a lot to say. I don't like him. But I'm not afraid of him anymore. I know his wicked ways.

I also know that, as Thomas More said of the devil, he "cannot bear to be mocked." Laughter is a fairly reliable antidote to self-defeating messages. Anne Lamott's freewheeling advice to writers to embrace their "shitty first drafts" offers cheerful, disarming acquiescence as a strategy for getting through what seems to be a predictable stage in creative work of any kind. Acknowledging imperfection, unfinishedness, messiness, and moving on keeps the critic in his/her place. Giving the critic a comic name and identity can help too. He/she isn't an avenging angel, but probably someone more like a tight-lipped middle-manager or a nosy, negative neighbor.

But it's also true that the inner critic may have a good point or two. He/she may be reminding you of besetting, self-defeating tendencies you actually need to recognize and avoid. Like the police, he/she may well be your "friend" as well as the one lying in wait to give you a ticket and spoil your trip.

I think of how Jesus taught and trained Peter—what a range of corrections, consolations, admonitions, and affirmations he offered his most memorable disciple. "Get thee behind me, Satan!" is a stingingly harsh word to the one he also called "the Rock." Peter's growth from "little faith" to impulsive enthusiasm to bewilderment, and finally to profound empowerment as a preacher and healer—this is a good story to recall when the inner critic appears. Peter was trained by the best of teachers. And all his training led him to a confidence as wide and deep as the humility and gratitude by which it was sustained.

—

Thursday: Dare to protest abuse of power

For peace of mind I suspect most of us suppress at least some of the grim political and economic realities we live with. Not only the increased incidence of drought and deluge, but the ways multinational corporations and military leaders put us at risk with high-level dice games even as they claim to provide and protect, are troubling indeed. Nine countries in the world possess over 15,000 nuclear weapons—the U.S. most of them—enough to destroy the planet many times over. All of us who live with that awareness probably share some degree of fatalism and some measure of fear about the scope and costs of war, nuclear accidents, and mad scientists in the grip of megalomania.

People of faith are called to act in the world for peace, justice, proper care of the earth, and proper care of each other. People of faith are doing just that every day—visiting prisons, showing up in combat zones to stand with the endangered, feeding the hungry, educating those imprisoned in ignorance, attending the dying, circulating petitions, writing legislation, offering safe havens.

What Paul called "principalities and powers" have always been in some ways beyond the control of ordinary citizens, even in functional democracies, and driven by private agendas at least as much as by concern for the common good. Despite our best efforts, things will very likely continue to happen that serve the interests of the powerful and harm the poor. So we make those efforts not because we think we can save the world, but because we're committed to living faithfully.

We're also committed to think beyond the political and even the planetary "boxes" we live in. In order not to be afraid of those among the powerful who seem willing to put us at risk, we have to remember at every turn that this world is not our home, that death is not the end, that the kingdom of heaven is already among us, and that our hope is sure and certain. That is the larger, truer story, the one we live by, that calls us, after all, to a joy that will one day be complete.

Friday: Dare to speak when it's called for

A university study of common fears conducted a few years back revealed the startling fact that fear of death took second place after fear of public speaking. Speaking *up*, speaking *out*, speaking *for*—all require a sense of vocation and discernment about when to break silence. Silence can be powerful—and tempting. It can be an act of prudence or of cowardly complicity. Sometimes justice requires us to speak.

It's hard to speak up or speak out if you're conflict-averse. Or if taking a public position is likely to draw you into a prolonged controversy for which you have limited time or energy. Or if you're exposing yourself to real repercussions—even danger. It's hard to speak out if your cohort of friends and family don't agree with you and you feel you'd risk damaging your relationship with your primary support group. It's also hard to speak up or speak out if you don't have all the facts, though it's good to remember that we never have all the facts, and to consider when evidence is both "sufficient" and "compelling." And it can be hard to speak up or speak out when it seems like that's someone else's job.

But sometimes the unavoidable fact is that it *is* our job. We're the ones called into the moment when a word needs to be said to clarify or defend or challenge or correct. Maybe there's no one else there. Or no one else has come forward with the relevant facts. Or others seem to be missing a crucial point. Or others don't recognize what's at risk. Or other speakers are doing harm.

There's certainly no dearth of people ready and willing to stand up and speak. But not all of them are speaking to good purpose; much public speaking serves private agendas, sows confusion, deceives for profit, or entertains without adequate care for truth. And sometimes silent disregard is the most appropriate response to pointless or irresponsible blather. If we took on every talk-show host who perpetuated unhelpful myths or distracting drivel, we might well squander our own precious hours to no particular avail. But certain kinds of slander, gossip, or misrepresentation need an answer.

And those who have no public voice need someone to speak for them. Undocumented immigrant children need advocates in the school system. Innocent people held in detention centers need public defenders. People who have lost pensions or jobs or homes without recourse need representation. Unpopular kids who are getting bullied in schoolyards need adults willing to intervene.

Speaking up and out and for is a measure of social and spiritual maturity. It's a condition of membership in the community, in the body. Some of us who think ourselves least likely to speak will sometimes need to rise and say the prophetic word. And some will, just as effectively, be driven to our knees, in private places, to speak the prayers for which others cannot find the words.

———

Saturday: Dare to endure what you must

In her book *Bearing the Unbearable: Trauma, Gospel, and Pastoral Care*, Deborah Hunsinger encourages Christian caregivers not to underestimate the damage that souls can suffer from physical and psychological trauma, or to short-circuit the lament or mourning that comes in their wake. Sustaining hope in the hardest of times can only be faithfully accomplished if no part of the suffering is glossed over, suppressed, or denied. The Gospel, she reminds us, is capacious enough to contain the full extent of human suffering. So caregivers need not shy away from the challenge of bringing hope into places of acute pain as long as the hope they bring is drawn from the deepest and purest well.

Hope that there will be a meaning and an end to suffering does not obviate consuming moments of overwhelming, wracking pain or grief. I find the lines at the end of Randall Jarrell's poem "90 North" oddly comforting simply for their bald factuality: "Pain comes from the darkness/And we call it wisdom. It is pain." These are not words of comfort or hope except to the extent that telling the truth about suffering is its own powerful form of comfort.

One of the great truths about suffering is that human beings have always endured it, both the ills that flesh is heir to and the atrocities we wreak upon one another at our worst. We all pray to be spared suffering, most of us, I imagine, believing with Thomas More that we are "not the stuff martyrs are made of." But we are, actually. What the martyrs had that we do not is the grace given in the moment to endure what they had to.

William Faulkner made broad claims for our capacity to endure in his 1950 Nobel acceptance speech. The task of the writer, he believed, was to "help man endure by lifting his heart, by reminding him of the courage and honor and hope and pride and compassion and pity and sacrifice which have been the glory of his past." Indeed, endurance was one of the great themes of his work. Faulkner ended his speech with this stirring claim: "I believe that man will not merely endure: he will prevail . . . because he has a soul, a spirit capable of compassion and sacrifice and endurance." While it falls short of the Gospel message of a grace that enables us to endure and a strength we can rely on that is beyond our own capacities, his affirmation is a reminder that we can and do, in fact, withstand more than we imagine, and that we are well equipped for this arduous, often dangerous journey.

"I will both lay me down in peace and sleep," the Psalmist writes, "for thou, Lord, only makest me dwell in safety." The place of peace lies in the very midst of the storm, in the only stronghold in which we are secure. That security is no stay against suffering, but an assurance that when we need to endure, we will be able.

Leave

. . . *yesterday behind*

. . . *father and mother*

. . . *what fosters no love*

. . . *what has served its purpose*

. . . *the table when you're full*

. . . *when it's time to rest*

. . . *the results to God*

Sunday: Leave yesterday behind

Barry Stevens, a psychologist popular in my youth, wrote a line I've found useful over the years: "Don't curl your toes over the past; all your energies are needed for the present." This idea is hardly original—we find a version of it in every wisdom tradition. But I like the phrase "curling one's toes," with its vivid reminder of what it's like to hang on to something—a surfboard, a foothold, a ladder rung, one's rising temper—to maintain a sense of security or control.

Curling our toes over the past is a way of clinging to the known and resisting the unknown. "We've always done it this way." "I can't get rid of these things; they were my mother's." "I'll never forgive myself (or him, or her, or them)." "My problems come from a difficult childhood." All of these assertions are fairly common ways of seeking help, explanation, or exoneration in the past.

But the past is a sticky place; the paths we trace through it get muddy and overgrown with unreliable memories and entangled associations. The gift of memory can become a curse; in biblical literature it cuts both ways. God remembers his covenant with Israel and is faithful. The Israelites are exhorted to "remember the whole way that the Lord your God has led you. . . ." Joseph, remembering a dream, brings about a historic reconciliation. Jesus reminds his followers to remember those in prison.

But forgetting has its place. Affirming the new covenant, God promises, "I will be merciful toward their iniquities, and I will remember their sins no more." Joseph gives thanks that "God has made me forget all my hardship. . . ." And Paul urges the Philippians to consider his own acceptance of God's forgiveness as a model, "forgetting what lies behind and straining forward to what lies ahead, [pressing] onward toward the goal for the prize of the upward call of God in Christ Jesus."

In some ways the past is inescapable. William Faulkner famously insisted, "The past is never dead. It's not even past." We carry it in our psyches and display it on our walls in family photographs that proclaim their half-truths, and we reveal it in the stories we tell now, into which the past bleeds like dye in water. But the freedom we receive as people released by forgiveness gives us permission to loose ourselves from bondage to the past and occupy the present with all our energies—open hearts, focused eyes and ears, attentive minds—consenting to the call of the moment, doing "whatsoever our hand findeth to do" with all our might.

One of Jesus' hard sayings is his instruction to "Let the dead bury the dead"—as strong a "leave the past behind" message as I know. It's spoken to a would-be disciple who's postponing following Jesus until his father dies so that he can be there to bury him. He was a dutiful young man. But when duty prevents the spontaneity we are invited to exercise in God's service, it becomes legalism.

It may be that the best image of healthy relationship to the past is fly fishing: catch and release. Remember and release. When the past offers lessons, receive them. When it debilitates or distracts, release it.

God meets us now. Here. New every morning. As Mary

Oliver puts it in "Morning Poem," "Every morning/the world/is created." There's no "again" in that sentence. In God we are invited into a place where "all is always now."

———

Monday: Leave father and mother

We hear it at every traditional Christian wedding: "Therefore a man shall leave his father and his mother and hold fast to his wife, and they shall become one flesh." Hard words for some of the parents sitting in the front row, though to judge from ensuing negotiations about where to spend holidays and how often to call, there are those who privately add modifying clauses to this redrawn social contract.

"Honor your father and your mother" is right there in the Ten Commandments, but how we are to live that out among the demands of adult life is ambiguous at best. What we owe our parents and elders isn't nearly as clear in middle-class North America as it is in some traditional cultures. Even those who share common roots in the biblical story find themselves on a broad and confusing spectrum of opinion about "family values" and the limits of parenting and elder care. By some measures the nuclear family is a historical disaster, leaving many women isolated with small children and no gathering space where the village helps raise them. The extended family, with all its competing needs, officious aunties, and eccentric uncles, has been far more normative and sturdy than the small suburban family unit, but those big gaggles of family folk have their shadow side too.

Jesus called his disciples to leave their families for substantial periods of time, and to put both livelihood and relatives at some risk in doing so. Many people are still called to such partings. When the work we are given to do involves relocation, travel, sabbatical retreats, or even a closed study door, it may be fitting and right to leave, for a time, even those who have the most intimate claims on us. I think of a friend whose daughter is an astronaut; she travels to Houston to watch that child disappear into space, each launch an exercise of radical trust. I think of my mother, who at twenty-four followed the Spirit's call to India, leaving her widowed mother and her sister to work at a school for orphans 8,000 miles away. I think of the long periods in my own life when, following a sometimes wayward path, I lived and worked far from the parents who would have loved to see more of me. But I'm also aware of how much grace was granted to all of us in those absences.

"Who is my mother?" Jesus asks, rather harshly, we may think, when she sends for him. "Who are my brothers?" And, indicating the crowds of followers, he provides the answer: "Whoever does the will of God, he is my brother and sister and mother."

Clearly Jesus had his own version of family values. We have every indication that he loved his mother, but in a way that left no question about what it means to claim the life he was called to, obedient first of all to the summoning of the Spirit, who comes on the wings of the morning and bears us up and away from the nest.

Tuesday: Leave what fosters no love

I remember the time I heard writer Stephen Levine speak to a group of people who had gathered to learn how to live with their suffering. Among other strong and simple words of encouragement he offered were these, to a woman who had subjected herself for years, under the guise of duty, to an oppressive and humiliating family: "You don't have to stay in an abusive situation." He went on to make the important distinction between the suffering we may be called to endure and the suffering we bring on ourselves by refusing to release ourselves from it.

The distinction between those two isn't always easy to make, particularly when it involves marriage vows, children, abuse that is a feature of mental illness, staying with people who clearly need help. But as a rule of thumb, loveless relationships—those that humiliate, deplete emotional energy, and exhaust the spirit—are a temptation we may need to resist. I call them a temptation because submission to certain forms of abuse, especially from family, all too often hooks people of faith who have big hearts, but not very big shields, and sometimes mistake low self-esteem for humility. Among the questions that can help assess the true nature of a relationship are these: "Is staying in this situation teaching me anything about love? Is it helping me become a more loving person? Is it allowing me to give and receive the grace, peace, and love of God?"

Where we have a choice in the matter, we have a responsibility to spend some time in discernment. Leaving may look cowardly, but be the most courageous choice. Leaving a place that fosters no love for a place that holds some promise of doing so may be the act of trust that God has been waiting for. There are no prescriptions here, but certainly some good guidelines. One is to reframe the question, asking "Where is God's invitation?" before asking "Should I leave?" Another is to remember Paul's frequent references to the joy he found in the sufferings he was called to. "Called to" being the key. We are assured that if we must, we can: grace will be given for what we must endure.

But when we endure unnecessary suffering—degrading work situations, for instance, or manipulative "friendships" that sap our energies and exploit good will—we need to ask whether it is fidelity or timidity that motivates us to keep submitting. To raise the question is not to indulge in self-serving rationalization, but rather to hold these behaviors, along with others, in God's light, and ask for guidance that might actually lead toward an escape route rather than into prolonged pain.

In such reflections I have found both unsettling and helpful a phrase from "Little Gidding" by T. S. Eliot: he speaks of "things ill done or done to others' harm/which once you took for exercise of virtue." From time to time it is good practice to submit even our "virtues" to examination of conscience, asking for clarity concerning what serves our deepest purposes, and God's. And to leave behind what does not.

Wednesday: Leave what has served its purpose

A rather inconspicuous line in T. S. Eliot's "Little Gidding" has often been helpful to me as an instrument of discernment: "These things have served their purpose: let them be." The speaker refers to "thoughts and theories" he once proclaimed that need not be rehearsed again; the moment in which they were needed has passed, and new "thoughts and theories" may be called for.

A meaningful exchange or game-changing idea or valuable practice—an eating regimen, an exercise routine, a particular form of daily devotion, a weekly lunch date—may be just what we need for a situation or a season, but when we pour concrete around those little flames of life energy, we're likely to snuff them out. Asking ourselves at regular intervals what purposes they're serving—the routines and practices and voluntary commitments—is itself a useful practice.

Years ago my husband and I went to a weekend marriage workshop. We and the other couples were asked to answer a particularly interesting and challenging question: not "Why did you choose each other in the first place?" but "Why do you want to keep living with each other?" It was an invitation to revisit our vows and bring them into the present. The point was not to question their value, but to recognize that they might serve new purposes in a new season, and might need rewording or reinterpretation.

For years of my life of teaching college English, I rotated into the freshman composition courses, where much of the work, as I saw it, was to gently pry students away from the securities of the prefab five-paragraph essay they had learned to write in high school. When you're fifteen, it's a valuable device for organizing ideas. When you're nineteen, it proves to be an inadequate vehicle for the ambiguities and complex definitions and digressions of adult life. It has served its purpose. But getting some of my students to leave it and move on into new strategies of argument or deeper waters of reflection required an ample supply of red ink. It's hard to leave what you know, what has served simpler purposes in a simpler time, what has felt safe.

Part of my morning prayer is that I be kept aware of and attentive to my deepest purposes, which reveal themselves in God's good time. Yesterday's manna is no longer fit to eat. And if I want a share of today's good wine, I'll need to be ready with new wineskins.

Thursday: Leave the table when you're full

I write this line with a nod of acknowledgment to every writer of the diet books I've encountered—and they are many. "Stop when you've had enough" seems to be an inescapable prerequisite to healthy and happy life in the body. The roots of this advice lie in two prescriptions attributed to a Buddhist teacher, though one might call them common sense: "Eat when you're hungry. Sleep when you're tired." These are deceptively simple precepts, especially in a culture that provides every incentive to ignore the body's signals and press on through twelve-hour workdays and 1200-calorie business dinners.

When overeating becomes normal, knowing when you're full, or when you're actually hungry, isn't so easy. The fact that 93 million Americans are affected by obesity suggests that the wisdom of our bodies is being drowned out by the plethora of social inducements to eat for all the wrong reasons. In this climate it's easy to lose a sense of personal responsibility or control over what and how much we eat. The consequences of that loss are sobering: not only poor health, but also reduced self-esteem and spiritual vitality.

In every culture I know of, meals have a sacred dimension. They are preceded by moments of thanksgiving, accompanied by reminders to share with those in want, and prepared in very particular ways for sacred occasions. When harvests are plentiful, plenty is cause for celebration, and eating and drinking a form of delight. But in my experience the pleasures of plenty have been diminished by the ways we produce, market, and consume food. Too much high-fructose corn syrup and salt, too much fossil fuel expended in transporting exotic foods to places of privilege, too many empty calories, and numerous animals raised cruelly for slaughter make North American meals occasions for ethical unease, if we're attentive to the costs of our pleasures and privilege.

So what we do at mealtime matters; a thousand threads

of cause and effect connect us there to other people's stories. We can't solve all the problems of the food systems we inhabit, but we can recognize that our eating practices are one way we live our faith in a God who provides and who established natural processes that are good and not to be violated. My personal stewardship of that provision begins in praying for the humility and wisdom to say "enough," feasting and fasting in due season for the right reasons, and seeking to understand, in a complex global economy, what is my share to claim and enjoy and when, by dint of greed, abundance is no longer a blessing.

—————

Friday: Leave when it's time to rest

Fatigue is a valuable teacher. It humbles me; it makes me aware of my limits. It makes me aware that I need others' help. It often directs me away from fruitless occupations that may appear to matter, but don't. I've done my share of "all-nighters" in efforts to meet deadlines and have borne the costs of over-commitment in hours I needed for rest and energy I drew from severely diminished supplies. The lessons fatigue teaches have, for me, been hard-won, but I am grateful for them.

I remember being struck by the courage and clarity it took for a colleague to ask, in the midst of a lengthy committee meeting with a long agenda, "When are we going to stop rewarding each other for doing too much?" She was challenging institutional norms and expectations too many of us found onerous and exhausting that were masked by accolades for diligence and productivity. "Tireless" has become a term of praise, and long hours a common measure of dedication rather than of consensual abuse.

Most of the Christians I know honor the invitation to Sabbath rest by attending worship and spending time with their families or friends, but most—myself included—also find the Sabbath a convenient day to catch up on work. One unusual and lovely couple I know hasn't succumbed to that erosion. The two of them play. They don't take any work-related calls. They read aloud and go on walks. And they rest. Unabashedly, joyfully, they take naps or sit by the window and gaze at the weather. They play board games with the kids.

Such leisure is, of course, also a function of privilege; people who work three jobs to feed their families have little choice in the matter of finding rest. But here I speak to those for whom rest is an option to suggest that if it's an option, it's also an obligation. In rest lies renewal. In rest we may become more receptive, reflective, and resilient.

To rest, we must relinquish the delusion that we're indispensable. We are not—any of us. If I got very sick tomorrow and was unable to do my work, I imagine that the world would shuffle on rather well without me. "God doth not need either man's work or his own gifts," Milton wrote in his famous poem on his blindness. Our work matters, but it isn't necessary. In it we are given the privilege of participating in the divine dance of creativity while we are in this world. But rest reminds us that what needs to happen will happen with or without our strenuous effort.

So I admire people with the courage to say, "I'll leave you all for a while. I'm going to take a nap." I'm not often among them. But I suspect that those naps—little acts of practical trust—bring with them not only refreshment for the remainder of the day, but their own particular blessing.

———

Saturday: Leave the results to God

It's tempting to be a poll-reader and a pulse-taker—one of those people who compulsively check on outcomes, measure them, crunch them into data, and recalculate. But thinking that we can control the outcome of what we do is, beyond a certain point, pointless. Our call as people of faith is to do what we do with our whole heart and best effort and leave the rest to God. The notion that we can do anything more than that is a little silly.

The metaphor of sowing seeds is a common one that preachers and teachers reach for to describe their work. Parents also know that though their efforts matter immensely, they can't possibly predict how or to what extent what they have modeled and advised will bear fruit in their children's lives. For farmers, of course, sowing, watching, and waiting are not metaphors. They may enrich the soil, rotate crops, compensate for weather cycles, compost, mulch, and experiment with new strains, but ultimately the harvest is out of their hands. Much contemporary "scientific" farming, drenched in fossil fuels and plumes of pesticide, is driven by complex knowledge applied with questionable wisdom.

I've been a writer for many years, but I'm often surprised—still—when someone I don't know writes to me about something I've written. Each of these communications is a reminder that what I write will be heard in circumstances and in ways I cannot predict. And it's the same for all of us. The architect can't control what use will be made of the spaces she designs. The microbiologist can't control the ways in which his research may be applied. The artist can't control where the patron hangs the painting. All of our efforts are offerings. The best we can do is send our gifts out with a prayer that they do no harm, and some good, in ways and places we can't know about—and need not know.

Welcome

... *the day*

... *the stranger*

... *correction*

... *change*

... *the new season*

... *the thing you fear*

... *the little ones*

Sunday: Welcome the day

As a "morning person" who takes particular pleasure in coffee by candlelight in the wee hours, I don't think I can claim any credit for virtue in early rising; it seems more an indulgence than, as some might find it, a moment of heroically forgoing another happy hour of burrowing under the quilt.

My husband, also a morning person, often joins me in the morning quiet. He does get some "virtue points" for making the coffee. Reading the lectionary passages aloud and sharing twenty minutes of quiet centering prayer send us into our separate days in peace and hope.

To the night-owls who find the early hours challenging at best, I offer my admiration for all the creative ways they find to make use of their own quiet times. And I extend my sympathies to them for the merciless ways the working day fails to accommodate their biorhythms.

To those at both ends of this circadian spectrum, I recommend the Welcoming Prayer as an aid to contemplative practice. Its first line is an emphatic repetition: "Welcome, welcome, welcome." The one who prays this prayer affirms an attitude or posture of welcome, a little like a yoga stretch that opens body and mind to the energies of earth and sky.

The second line gets more specific, and scarier: "I welcome everything that comes to me today." The line in the prayer doesn't end with a period, but it does end, inviting us to pause for a moment and take in the enormity of that simple act of trust. "Everything" covers a lot of eventualities, some of which any sane person would want to avoid. "Everything" suggests the kind of radical confidence I have always found inspiring in Psalm 139, with its lovely cascade of lines reminding us of how God shows up, even at "the uttermost parts of the sea," even if I "make my bed in hell." And so, the prayer reminds us, whatever comes to us today, God will get there first.

The next line adds a dimension to the broad welcome already uttered: I welcome everything that comes "because I know it's for my healing." Even what hurts. Or inconveniences, or annoys, or puzzles, or reconfigures our plans. Reframing happenstance in this rather counter-rational way is a vigorous act of practical faith similar to an exercise often taught in improvisation classes for actors: whatever happens on stage, say yes to it and respond. Say "Yes, and . . ." Move into the "yes" with an action that invites others in.

The Welcoming Prayer continues with a series of increasingly bold specifics: "I welcome all thoughts, feelings, emotions, persons, situations, and conditions." And then come the let-gos: "I let go of my desire for power and control, for affection, esteem, approval, pleasure, survival, security. . . ." In a way, all this relinquishment begins the day with death to the self that clings and limits and resists.

This, I think, is what it looks like to choose life, stepping onto the stage with a bold "Yes" and welcoming what comes. Because, if we really understand how ultimately secure we are in the context of the cosmic story we inhabit, we know we can afford that "yes," undisturbed and unafraid because God is with us.

Monday: Welcome the stranger

As I write this, an estimated nine million Syrian refugees have fled their homes to escape civil war in their homeland, desperate for food, water, and safety, watching children starve, challenging the charity and the emergency resources of neighboring countries. Refugees from hostile governments, from entrapment in crushing poverty and political threats cross borders every day.

And the immigration debate goes on. To whom do we give political asylum? Green cards? Citizenship? Drivers' licenses? Medical care? Basic education? Just what do we owe our poorer neighbors?—a question that seems to hit a very different visceral spot when it's asked of us collectively. The leap from personal moral standards and practices and what we support politically is sometimes surprisingly long.

The ethic of hospitality in both Old and New Testaments includes strong, clear admonitions to welcome strangers, never forgetting that we might find ourselves wayfarers one day; that welcome is both generous and prudent—a reasonable alternative to desperate violence and border wars; and that we might, as the writers of Hebrews remind us, be entertaining angels, unaware. It's easy to piously accept this teaching in the abstract, but when it becomes a practical matter of opening the doors to our church's multipurpose room or to our living rooms, welcoming strangers gets complicated. Most of us in North American cities and suburbs are all too aware of the threat of violent crime to be comfortable opening doors to any but those we know and trust. In many neighborhoods it would be imprudent and foolish to do so.

We need one another to help us safely provide the safety others need. We need help identifying needs—food, to be sure, and clothes and a warm shower, and a simple manicure and a conversation, and a bed for the night and a bit of privacy. We need help moving beyond the fear that keeps us from making eye contact and speaking the word of greeting someone might not have heard for hours or days. And we need to go back to where we might see the stranger again, and ask her name.

"Welcome" comes from an early English word meaning "one whose coming brings pleasure." To welcome the stranger is to remember what pleasure may be taken when our paths intersect with others', that even strange and unsettling others may become our teachers, and that love has a thousand faces, some of them unwashed.

Tuesday: Welcome correction

I once expressed admiration for a friend who seemed unusually gracious and thoughtful about accepting criticism. Her response to my compliments has been a helpful word over the years when I've been on the receiving end of others' judgments, criticisms, and corrections: "I've just found that it's liberating not to have to defend yourself." "Liberating" caught my attention. She wasn't preaching patience or humility, though those are worth cultivating; she wasn't saying her critics were right. She seemed rather to have discovered a spaciousness of heart and a quiet confidence that could afford to entertain others' opinions without either capitulation or resistance.

"Hmm. I'll have to think about that," I heard her say more than once to people who freely offered what seemed to me rather petty judgments. Sometimes she added "Thank you" without a trace of irony, and went her own way. Sometimes she took their advice; sometimes she didn't. She seemed to me a model of mental health sustained by a generous spirit.

She was and is a woman of deep faith. One of the strengths her faith provides is security in knowing herself to be unconditionally loved and freely forgiven. So correction and criticism are not threats to her self-esteem, her self-image, her self-confidence. She can afford to listen and consider. She can afford to change if change is called for, freely and without fear of entering a spiral of shame.

I have thought of her not only when I've received correction, but when I've given it. In a long teaching career, I've spent a good gallon of red ink on corrections—efforts to redirect students' arguments or encourage greater specificity or insist on more precise fact-checking. Their responses, when I review their papers with them, range from passive to meek to eager to please, from genuinely thoughtful and eager to learn to discerning and imaginative. Giving correction is gratifying in those instances when it provides an occasion for inventively revisiting possibilities, rewriting paragraphs, rethinking an approach to a problem, and in the process finding our way into rich, reflective conversation that is life-giving for both of us. Those conversations are the ones teachers often refer to when they say, as many do, "I find that I learn as much from my students as they do from me."

Those students, like my friend who learned how to make a gift of correction, have taught me what grace lies in openness to correction. "Teach me your paths," the Psalmist writes. "Lead me in your truth." "Correct me, O Lord," Jeremiah prays. And the writer of Proverbs assures us, "The Lord reproves him whom he loves."

Not all correction comes from above; some of it comes from jealousy, envy, or a fussy need to control. But even that correction, if we welcome it with generosity and good humor, may deliver its grain of truth to add to our store of wisdom. And it may well be, as T. S. Eliot suggested, that "the only wisdom we can hope to acquire is the wisdom of humility," indicating, as I understand him, that humility (a word related to *humus*, earth) is the ground in which all other virtues grow.

———

Wednesday: Welcome change

The sign on a tip jar at a local café counter never fails to make me smile: "If you fear change, leave it here." I've never seen the jar empty. Apparently many of us do fear change. In fact, a recent article in the *Harvard Business Review* listed ten reasons people resist change, including loss of control, disruption of habits, and the fact that change involves more work and a loss of a sense of competence. People will sometimes choose even what is unpleasantly familiar over what promises relief, growth, and pleasure.

We've all been there, I imagine—stayed in a job or home or social group or project long beyond the point where it ceased to provide satisfaction, or ignored increasingly evident signals that it's time to take a leap of faith into a new circumstance and acknowledge that we're in a new season.

Change in itself is neither good nor bad. When the opportunity to change comes, continuity and stability need to be weighed against the promise of growth, novelty, and challenge that lead us to consider venturing into untried waters. Sometimes we can test the water to see if it's safe. Sometimes the only way to get into it is to dive. It's the diving that's hard.

I came upon a poem by W. H. Auden years ago when I was facing exactly that kind of decision—to stay or take a dive into the unknown, or, as I now see it, a leap of faith. The poem, entitled "Leap before You Look," begins with a startling challenge:

Our sense of danger must not disappear:
The way is certainly both short and steep,
However gradual it looks from here;
Look if you like, but you will have to leap.

The last line concludes with similar insistence: "Our dream of safety has to disappear." I've had many occasions to consider those paradoxes as personal choices have led me to discern more complicated understandings of fidelity (easily mistaken for simply sticking it out). Considering leaving a job I loved, for instance, led me to a rich period of reflection on what it was I was called to be faithful to—not, finally, the institution or the work I prepared for in graduate school, but a willingness to consent to the call of the moment, as honestly as I could discern that call. Not all my decisions to change have been wise, but as I've gotten older, more of them have involved me in deep conversations with myself, others, and God that have helped me not to cling to the side of the pool, or even the edge of the cliff, but to let go and say yes.

Recently I learned that the familiar, comforting line in Psalm 46, "Be still and know that I am God," can also be translated "Let go and know that I am God." Every time I manage to let go of the past and welcome what comes— new, different, unanticipated—and hold my plans with an open hand, I'm learning to live in trust and depend on prayer and discovering in myself resources and resilience that might otherwise remain hidden under a bushel.

Thursday: Welcome the new season

"For behold, the winter is past. . . ." This, among the loveliest lines in the Song of Solomon, summons the beloved into a new season:

The rain is over and gone. The flowers have already appeared in the land. The time has arrived for pruning the vines. And the voice of the turtledove has been heard in our land.

Those of us who work in climate-controlled buildings and buy "petroleum-drenched" food from supermarkets that import grapes from Chile, tomatoes from Mexico, and oranges from Australia have a diminished relationship to the seasons. Many of us, connecting the dots between our food system and climate change, are paying more attention to eating what is local and in season. This means that when summer squash is out of season, we let it go and look up recipes for cabbage and cauliflower around the same time we pack away the beach gear and get the parkas out of storage.

Welcoming a new season in a marriage or a career or a friendship or in the life of one's body may be harder. Little in the culture encourages us to rejoice in growing older, or in the gradual way passionate romance softens to familiar companionship, or in slowing down to accommodate a stressed knee or an aching hip. But sometimes what seems like a loss is preparation for new, subtler, unexpected satisfactions.

The morning I turned sixty, I woke up with a surprising sense of exhilaration, even excitement, at the dawn of a new decade. I didn't expect that. But I had a sense of entering a new season of life, able to be the "elder" that others had been for me, able to make new choices about using my days with a heightened sense of their preciousness, able to consider the question of what I want to do before I die with just a bit more urgency. It is, of course, poignant when you watch the door close on certain pleasures or opportunities. I still recall the moment my father shook his head when I asked him to carry me and said, "You're too big for that now. You can walk." I remember how the momentary sadness gave way to the unfamiliar pleasure in this small measure of independence.

Still, some seasons are dark indeed. It would be glib to suggest that we welcome a season of mourning or illness with gladness of heart. But even in those, as we find our way into a deeper acceptance, we may find that acceptance may grow into something more than reluctant concession. The grace available on what seem the worst days of our lives may be more abundant than any of us expects, and may teach us, in our sorrow, something new about hope.

Friday: Welcome the thing you fear

For a while my father-in-law took a great interest in the practice of "conscious dreaming"—what's often called "lucid dreaming." Either before sleep or during the dream itself, the dreamer can learn to participate in the action of the dream, sometimes symbolically working out problems he or she has been wrestling with in waking life.

With his encouragement, I did a bit of reading on the subject myself, and was rewarded twice with remarkable reassurances that empowered me to cope with besetting fears. One came in a recurrent dream in which I was running up a beach, panic-stricken, to escape a tidal wave. After years of waking from this distressing dream, there was the night that I saw the wave coming, and, rather than racing up the dunes toward safety, I turned and dove into the wave. I surfaced on the other side of it into peaceful waters glistening with sunlight. The wave broke high on the beach while I swam safely toward shore.

This particular image of facing fear would very likely be worthless in the event of an actual tidal wave, but it has served as a vivid reminder that the way out is sometimes in or through. The skier facing a steeper slope than she's tried before, the child riding the bike on his own, the speaker walking to a podium before an audience of strangers, the jury member preparing to cast the single dissenting vote, the woman calling an angry friend to work out a painful conflict—all face fears that could be paralyzing. I'm sure I'm not the only one who's had dreams of showing up at work unprepared or standing on a crumbling cliff or running from an armed pursuer. Waking or sleeping, fear is real, and always a challenge to discernment and an invitation to prayer.

When angels show up in biblical stories, they almost always open the conversation with "Be not afraid," no doubt because they're terrifying. Yet what they bring is good news, guidance, protection, reassurance. These fearsome messengers come to us, it seems, to help us leave our very human comfort zones and rise to the challenge of divine encounter.

The hard truths that face us all and that many would

prefer to avoid or deny—climate change, human trafficking, economic downturns, urban violence—are hardly to be welcomed in and of themselves. But every one of them may serve to sharpen our sense of interdependence and enliven our collective intelligence and political will to become what we are called to be.

"God does not leave us comfortless," writes Jane Kenyon in "Let Evening Come," a poem about facing her own death. And so she can afford to face it, and so we can trust that as in life and death we belong to God, even what we most fear may be a path of peace.

———

Saturday: Welcome the little ones

I imagine that we're all touched by Jesus' well-known welcome to children: "Let the little children come to me and do not hinder them, for to such belongs the kingdom of heaven." The lines that precede those gracious words are less often quoted: "Then some children were brought to him so that he might lay his hands on them and pray; and the disciples rebuked them."

At first hearing we might be inclined to wonder whether all that itinerant camping with stones for pillows and fish for breakfast had made the disciples more than usually irritable. Who would stop a little child from receiving a blessing? But a second hearing might remind us how hard it can be to welcome the inconveniences and interruptions that come with child care. All the bids for attention, the pleas to play crushingly boring board games, and the repeated requests for contraband sugar or prolonged playtime add up. There comes a point when we don't want to "suffer the little children," as the King James Version so aptly puts it.

It takes a village, as they say, to raise a child. But most of us don't live in social groups even remotely like villages, so we have to re-imagine ways to enfold families with children in churches and neighborhoods, offering support to single parents and serving as engaged elders for children who spend most of their lives in age-segregated schools, sports, and social situations. Some churches are deliberate about connecting older people with younger ones in local "family groups" who celebrate holidays and homework time together. Efforts like that take time and intention. Market forces apply powerful centrifugal pressure on families through video games and media images that routinely represent busy and preoccupied parents as problems for kids entrapped in complicated social landscapes at school or isolated in well-wired rooms at home.

Welcoming children means learning how to entice them into authentic conversation, sharing stories, laughing over riddles, perhaps making a little popcorn and watching *Frozen* again, holding them when they're sad, providing a safe space in which to ask about or report difficult things. These relationships don't happen automatically or by accident. Many children's lives are highly programmed. Sometimes we have to squeeze ourselves onto their calendars in order to spend time with them. But they need us—voices from a different generation who can provide perspective along with popcorn, who take them seriously, who pray for them, who play with them (even the more boring board games), who lure them into good books by reading aloud, who correct them kindly, and who provide space in our hearts and at our kitchen tables and time in our afternoons to sit with them and call them by name.

My husband and I have several friends who've been foster parents. Others volunteer their time every week at local schools, homework centers, and Boys' and Girls' Clubs. Others teach Sunday school or coach soccer or make costumes for plays. And some just open their doors and let in the neighborhood kids—gum, dirty running shoes, and all. Their homes are havens for children who need all the support they can get in the world they're required to navigate. They need blessing more than rebuke. And we need them to remind us, often in surprising and poignant ways, what the Kingdom of Heaven is made of.

RESOURCES

Sources for Further Instruction and Reflection on Lectio, on Centering Prayer, and on Words:

http://www.patheos.com/Resources/Additional
   -Resources/Praying-with-Scripture-06172009
http://www.lectio-divina.org
http://www.valyermo.com/ld-art.html
http://www.centeringprayer.com
Cynthia Bourgeault, *Centering Prayer and Inner Awakening*
M. Basil Pennington, *Centering Prayer: Renewing an Ancient Christian Prayer Form*

ABOUT THE AUTHOR

Marilyn McEntyre is a professor of literature and medical humanities, a frequent retreat speaker, an adult teacher and workshop leader, a hospice volunteer, and a writer. Much of her writing focuses on the role of words and language practices in the life of faith. Her recent books include *Caring for Words in a Culture of Lies*, *What's in a Phrase?*, *A Faithful Farewell*, and *A Long Letting Go*.